KT-226-740

Contents

Cliff +
Michelle.
c/o
kings Fellowship
Inverness
IV2 4JD.

Back in Time

Back in Time

A Thinking Fan's Guide to *Doctor Who*

Steve Couch, Tony Watkins and Peter S. Williams

Copyright © 2005 Steve Couch, Tony Watkins and Peter S. Williams

First published in 2005 by Damaris Books, an imprint of Authentic Media, 9 Holdom Avenue, Bletchley, Milton Keynes, Bucks, MK1 1QR, UK and 129 Mobilization Drive, Waynesboro, GA 30830-4575, USA.

The right of Steve Couch, Tony Watkins and Peter S. Williams to be identified as the authors of this work has been asserted by them in accordance with the Copyright, Designs and Patents Act 1988.

All rights reserved. No part of this publication may be reproduced or transmitted in any form or by any means, electronic or mechanical, including photocopy, recording or any information storage and retrieval system, without permission in writing from the publisher.

British Library Cataloguing in Publication Data

A catalogue record for this book is available from the British Library.

1-904753-09-4

Unless otherwise stated, all Scriptural quotations have been taken from the HOLY BIBLE, NEW INTERNATIONAL VERSION. Copyright © 1973, 1978, 1984 by the International Bible Society. Used by permission of Hodder & Stoughton, a member of Hodder Headline Ltd. All rights reserved.

Print management by Adare Carwin
Typeset by GCS, Leighton Buzzard, Beds. in 11 on 13 Palatino
Printed in the UK by J.H. Haynes & Co., Sparkford

Introduction

These notes are being written on Friday 22 July 2005, a week prior to our deadline for this book and – more significantly – the day that filming starts on the 2006 series of *Doctor Who*.

The authors of this book are all long-standing *Doctor Who* fans of different vintages. Like countless others, we waited with breathless anticipation as the days and weeks counted down to Saturday 26 March 2005, and the return of brand new *Doctor Who* to British television screens. We already knew that we wanted to write this book, but we would have been just as excited anyway.

This is a book that is written by *Doctor Who* fans for *Doctor Who* fans. Our aim is to add to your appreciation of one of the most distinctive, original and long-running shows in television history, and to help you to think more clearly about some of the themes and issues that run through the show. We have tried to write a book that will help new fans to discover the heritage of previous versions of *Doctor Who*, and also remind longer-standing fans of why we loved *Doctor Who* in the first place. Either way, the current show is firmly built on the foundation of the past, so a degree of looking back will be informative (and fun) for all of us.

The first part of this book focuses primarily on the phenomenon of the TV programme, while part two takes a closer look at some of the themes and issues that underpin the programme, such as humanity, death and much more. All three authors of this book are Christians. While much of the book, particularly part two, reflects a Christian perspective on the various themes and issues of *Doctor Who*, we are not assuming you share our beliefs. *Doctor Who* fans are more than familiar with disagreement. Debates rage as to which Doctor, or which adventure, is best, and which monster costumes the most ridiculous. We don't necessarily expect you to agree with our belief any more (or less) than we expect you to agree with our opinion about the relative merits of the various Doctors. For what it's worth, we disagree on that particular subject, with Patrick Troughton, Tom Baker and Christopher Eccleston fighting it out for first place. This is a book to help you think more clearly, and if our argument stimulates your thinking – whether you agree with us or not – we will feel that our time has been well spent.

We should add a word here about what we have counted as being authoritative *Doctor Who* and what has been put to one side. We have followed Russell T. Davies' lead in considering as canonical only those versions of *Doctor Who* which were made primarily for broadcast on BBC television. This means that the 1996 TV movie is included, whereas the various audio stories and new *Doctor Who* novels are not. It also means omitting the two 1960s *Doctor Who* movies starring Peter Cushing. Cushing's Doctor, while travelling in a TARDIS of classic *Who* design is nevertheless represented as being a human inventor rather than a Time Lord. This wasn't so much a deliberate change, as a filling in of the blanks that the TV show hadn't got round to yet (Time

Lords weren't introduced to the show until the final Patrick Troughton adventure in 1969). Nevertheless, the movies took the show in a different direction giving grounds for not accepting Cushing's portrayal as being the same character that was subsequently played by Christopher Eccleston. None of this should be seen as reflecting in any way on the quality of the *Doctor Who* tales in various media we have ignored, merely that a line had to be drawn somewhere, and Russell T. Davies seemed to be as good an authority as any to trust on this matter.

Not that *Doctor Who* has always been overly concerned with continuity. One *Doctor Who* script editor has described his approach to the subject as being limited to 'whatever I could remember of the other bloke's script'. The lengthy history of the show is riddled with mutually exclusive legends and contradictions that would confuse even proponents of multiple universes.

In the early days of *Doctor Who*, adventures which spanned more than one episode were not aired under a single title (in fact, audiences didn't even know how many episodes a story would last for, allowing for genuine surprises if the Doctor and his companions were returning to the TARDIS at the end of an episode, job apparently done, only for something scary to jump out of the bushes at them). We have referred to these stories by the overall title that they are most commonly associated with. We have also added the year of first broadcast as an aid for those who do not have an encyclopaedic recall of such details. If you see an episode title which isn't followed by a year, it is either one from the 2005 series, or one which has previously been referenced with the year earlier in the chapter. We should also point out that we are assuming that you have seen the 2005 series, so don't blame us for any plot spoiling information if you haven't.

There are a few people who we owe a debt of thanks to. Tony and Steve would like to thank their wives and children: Jane Watkins and Charlie, Ollie and Pip; Ann Couch and Peter. All of them have had to put up with a large disruption to family life during the writing of this book, and have remained supportive in spite of the difficulties that this has caused. Peter Williams on the other hand enjoys the bachelor life and had nobody to complain when he went to watch yet another old *Doctor Who* video.

Talking of videos, Louise Crook helped us to find some obscure William Hartnell episodes and Matt Roberts leant us a significant part of his *Doctor Who* collection, which has proved invaluable in our research (and a lot of fun too, although Jane Watkins and Ann Couch may disagree). Matt also read and commented on some early drafts of chapters, as did Mark Duggan who provided some exceptionally helpful observations. Emily Dalrymple arrived at the Damaris offices as a temporary researcher for our Tools For Talks website, and was subsequently poached by the authors to do some invaluable fact checking for us as well.

We would also like to thank our colleagues at the Damaris Trust for their support during this project, particularly in the final stages as we raced against our deadline with all the urgency of the Doctor racing to set up a Delta Wave. Thanks are also due to our partners at Authentic Media for their support on this book, and their willingness to trust us with such a tight schedule.

Steve and Peter would like to thank the people who attended their seminar on Science Fiction at the Christian Resources Exhibition at Sandown in May

2005, where some of the ideas contained in this book were given an airing.

Our thanks go to all these people, but as ever any faults that remain in the book are nobody's responsibility but our own. Unless, of course, Rose has been up to her Bad Wolf tricks again.

Steve Couch, Tony Watkins and Peter S. Williams
July 2005

Part One

1. A Brief History of Time Lords

The Doctor is a legend woven throughout history
Clive in 'Rose'

'We want it to be everything the old series was, with a great big wodge of 2005 shoved into it'.[1] With the benefit of hindsight, Russell T. Davies' description of his revived version of *Doctor Who* sums things up perfectly. A classic BBC format dating back to the 1960s (and all-but absent from our screens since 1989) became the must-see television show of the year. The loyal band of *Doctor Who* fans were, for the most part, delighted with the result, but a whole new audience was brought in too. Television's most famous time-travel drama had been brought spectacularly up to date.

The news of the Doctor's imminent return first broke in September 2003. Russell T. Davies was confirmed as the head writer and – alongside Mal Young and Julie Gardner – executive producer. Fan Internet discussion boards went into overdrive, expressing joy at the long-awaited revival of the show as well as fears that the new team would mess it all up, finally killing the Doctor off forever in the eyes of the BBC. Fortunately, the show was in the hands of a long-time fan.

Russell T. Davies cut his scriptwriting teeth in the acclaimed children's television show *Children's Ward*, before making a name as a controversial, yet strikingly intelligent writer with dramas like *The Second Coming* (starring Christopher Eccleston) and *Queer As Folk*. Mal Young describes Davies as able to make 'the popular smart and the smart popular',[2] and a look through his non-*Who* work shows a recurring tendency to produce accessible, popular work that retains an ability to raise and explore serious issues.

Restoring a Past Master

As Davies and the rest of the production team began the task of shaping the new *Doctor Who*, crucial decisions that would determine the direction of the show were made. The basic format, of a man who travelled through time and space fighting evil and righting wrongs, was retained. The famous theme tune was also retained in an updated score by series composer Murray Gold. The Doctor's ship, the TARDIS,[3] kept its shape as a blue, 1950s police telephone box. As before, a malfunctioning chameleon circuit has robbed the TARDIS of its ability to change appearance to suit its location. Originally thought up as a way of saving additional design work over the course of a long series, this helped to create one of the most iconic objects of the television age (even if, like Rose, many viewers are now too young to remember police telephone boxes in any context other than the TARDIS).

But some revisions were necessary to bring the format up to date. Out went the four-, five-, six- and even ten-episode adventures, to be replaced by single stand-alone episodes with a handful of two-part stories. Perhaps more significantly, Davies was clear that he wasn't writing just for the traditional fans:

I specifically set out to target women. I think you can guarantee that a lot of men will switch on just because it's science fiction and it's got Billie Piper in it. But we wanted more than that. We've had a lot of strong, female characters, a lot more emotion and a lot more fun. There's also none of that dull, military hardware side to it – that's a real turn-off.[4]

From the word go, the production team set out to make *Doctor Who* a genuine family show, appealing to more than just the die-hard fans who had kept the *Who* fires burning in the long, dark intermission of the soul. Davies doesn't see a place in the current series for a 'hard sci-fi' episode: 'The essence of early Saturday is to keep it simple. Which doesn't mean dumb . . . The important thing on Saturdays is to shout the headline. Dalek! Dickens! Blitz! Big Brother! A headline shouting "Interesting Exploration of Temporal Physics" isn't gonna work the same way.'[5] So, the new series has reinvigorated a classic TV format, but where did that format come from?

The Day of the Monsters

Doctor Who first appeared on our TV screen on 23 November 1963 (famously, the day after John F. Kennedy was assassinated – an event which is knowingly referenced in the first episode of the 2005 *Doctor Who*), the result of an attempt to fill a scheduling gap for Saturday teatime, between the sport of *Grandstand* and the pop music of *Juke-Box Jury*. The first man to take his place at the TARDIS's control console was William Hartnell, whose Doctor was older in appearance than any of his successors, and who played the time-traveller as an irascible, grumpy old man (according to writer Terrance Dicks, this was because Hartnell was an irascible, grumpy old man).[6]

The man most often credited as the father of *Doctor Who* is Sydney Newman, who became BBC television's Head of Drama in 1962. However, the lengthy success of *Doctor Who* was built on a move away from his original vision. Newman's intention was for a show which would always retain a strong factual core – stories set in Earth's history must be as accurate as possible in recreating the authentic costume and language of the day; stories set on other planets must reflect the best knowledge of those environments currently available. Above all, the show was to have a strong educational value – to be more science fact than science fiction. And Newman's number one taboo: there were to be no 'bug-eyed monsters'.

Clearly, the show has departed significantly from this initial concept, and it travelled a long way very quickly. In the first series, episodes were shot just a few weeks in advance of broadcast. Due to a number of unforeseen circumstances, when the first adventure 'An Unearthly Child' (1963) finished, the only story that was ready to follow it onto the screens was Terry Nation's 'The Daleks' (1963/64). At the end of episode one, a strange sucker-like device on a stick loomed into view as Barbara, one of the Doctor's assistants, cowered against a wall. The best-known monster in the history of television had arrived, bug-eye and all.

Newman, apparently, was livid. He accused producer Verity Lambert of betraying his conception of the show, turning it into precisely the gratuitously fantastical trash that he so disliked. He also recognised that he had no choice but to allow the other episodes of 'The Daleks' to be broadcast as scheduled. But it soon became clear that the strange metal creatures had struck a chord with a large number of people. When the viewing figures for the second episode (of seven) in the story were released, *Doctor Who* had gained an additional two and a half million viewers. Episode four gained a further million, and it wasn't long before Britain was deluged with children running around with saucepans on their heads shouting 'Exterminate!' at the top of their lungs.

The focus of *Doctor Who* had undergone a dramatic shift. Stories with a historical flavour would still appear – probably more so during William Hartnell's time than for any of his successors – but now the audience also expected an episode of *Doctor Who* to scare them. The show had come out of the classroom and crept decisively behind the sofa.

Eliminate the Wobble

The high production standards on the 2005 *Doctor Who* play a significant part in maintaining the fear factor. Referring to the classic show's reputation for insubstantial sets, Russell T. Davies personally promised to 'eliminate wobble'[7] from *Doctor Who*, leaning against sets himself if need be. Fortunately, such low-tech solutions were not necessary. Sixteen years is a long time in technology, and the development of Computer Generated Imagery (CGI) has revolutionised what is possible. Producers of the old version of the show must have watched their televisions with eyes greener than a Slitheen when they saw the massed ranks of the Dalek space fleet at the end of 'Bad Wolf', or the sheer variety of convincing aliens in 'The End of the World'. Visual effects producer Will Cohen reckons that the second episode alone included some 203 special effects shots –

twice as many as the film *Gladiator* (and shot in almost a tenth of the time).[8]

The old *Doctor Who* is often unfairly criticised for its special effects. Many scenes look dated – sometimes laughably so – when watched by today's sophisticated audience who are used to much higher standards. But in their day, many of the effects were groundbreaking and, given the budgetary constraints of a humble BBC drama show, cutting edge. One writer commented in 1983 that 'even the most casual viewers of *Doctor Who* can hardly have failed to be impressed by the elaborate futuristic sets, the authentic-looking technological equipment and the splendid costumes and props which all add extra dimensions to the Doctor's adventures.'[9] 'The Daemons' (1971) concludes with a village church being blown up. So convincing was the model-making at the time that there were letters of complaint that such a beautiful and historic building should be destroyed just for the sake of a children's television programme. Nevertheless, the new show is much better resourced, both in terms of what is technologically possible and in the relative size of budget that the BBC is willing to make available.

Delight and Despair

Two important announcements were made in the week following the triumphant first episode of 2005's version of *Doctor Who*. First of all, the BBC declared that they were commissioning an hour-long Christmas special as well as a second season. Secondly, Christopher Eccleston announced that he would not be continuing in the role of the Doctor.

Subsequently it has become apparent that Russell T. Davies was always aware of the possibility that Eccleston would leave after only one series, even if he wasn't sure that this would be the case. The question has been asked why did Davies and the BBC powers-that-be allow such a situation – why didn't they get their star signed up on a longer contract? Now that the show has been greeted with almost universal acclaim, it is easy to underestimate the BBC's very real fear of the show falling flat. Davies has commented that with press speculation linking the likes of Paul Daniels and Ainsley Harriot with the role, 'we absolutely had to get one of the best actors in the land.'[10] Casting an actor of Eccleston's calibre gave *Doctor Who* a credibility with the unconverted that played a significant part in attracting publicity and winning a huge, popular audience. A less well-known actor, however talented, may have lacked the profile to establish the series after such a lengthy break, but could be ideal to step into Eccleston's shoes once the show was a success.

Nevertheless, many fans of the show were devastated that Eccleston was to leave so soon. Internet discussion boards were flooded with comments, many of which expressed a sense of betrayal. Back in March 2005, with only one episode of the new era in the public domain, many were – once again – fearing for the future of the show.

To some extent, this had echoes of a previous stage in the show's history.

Reborn to Run and Run

William Hartnell's health had troubled him for much of his time in the TARDIS. The production schedule was gruelling, and his arteriosclerosis meant that he consistently struggled with learning lines. Also, since the departure of all of his original on-screen companions, as well as several key members of the production team, Hartnell was enjoying the work less and less, and arguing in rehearsal more and more. Only the fear of being the man who killed off a show that meant so much to so many children held him back from making the break.

Hartnell agreed to return for the beginning of a fourth series, and the search began for a solution that would allow the show to go on without him, and for the right actor to step into his shoes. The solution lay in the Doctor's alien nature. Rather than simply swap actors and hope nobody noticed, or have the Doctor leave and a new time traveller take his place, the decision was made that the Doctor's race should have the ability to regenerate when their bodies became worn out. The now famous regeneration sequence was achieved by filming both actors against matching scenery, and cross-fading the film from one to the other.

We have become used to the effect of one Doctor fading out and another fading in to take his place, but on 29 October 1966, it was a whole new world for the excited audience. The following week, Patrick Troughton was to make his debut proper as the Doctor, and with the help of a first story facing the ever-popular Daleks, he was up and running with a fresh perspective on the character. There was no scientific (or even pseudo-scientific) explanation for the change of appearance, simply a comment from the new-look Doctor to his mystified companions Ben and Polly that he had 'rejuvenated' himself. A bold and innovative piece of television history not only enabled *Doctor Who* to survive the loss of its leading man, it also created the possibility of a show with the potential to run indefinitely.

Patrick Troughton was well known and respected as a character actor, ideally suited to the challenge of subtly incorporating elements of Hartnell's character into his own portrayal of the Doctor, while also making sure that he brought something new and distinctive to the role. It has often been said that in the hands of a lesser actor, the show would have died in 1966 or soon after. Hartnell himself approved of the casting at the time, and is reported to have commented subsequently that Troughton was the only man in the country who could have pulled it off. Nevertheless, Troughton had his doubts, and has said that he only expected the show to last six weeks or so once he took over.

One obvious difference between the first two Doctors was that Troughton literally rejuvenated the character – he was 12 years younger and more energetic than his predecessor. More than this, where Hartnell was patrician and authoritarian, Troughton was impish and playful. The phrase most commonly associated with Troughton's Doctor is 'cosmic hobo'. Indeed the inspiration for Troughton's costume reputedly came from Sydney Newman's instruction to 'Make him Chaplin! Make him a goddam hobo of the skies!'[11]

Golden Years

The handover from Hartnell to Troughton proved an enormous success, and was to be the first of many such changes, which served to show a different facet of the Doctor's character and generally freshen up the show every few years.

Next into the TARDIS was Jon Pertwee in 1970.

Pertwee had forged a reputation as a comic actor on radio and in films. He played the Doctor very much against this stereotype – his is possibly the straightest interpretation of the character, with less comic business or humour than any of the other Doctors. Pertwee's arrival also marked two significant changes to the format and production of the show.

First of all, the show moved over to colour, where previously it had always been recorded in black and white. At the time this was a striking new addition, but in retrospect, Troughton's monochrome episodes retain a more potent ability to scare than the Technicolor offerings of the early 70s, which can show up more harshly the limited budget for monster costumes and special effects.

The added cost of colour filming also led to the second change: the Doctor's travels would be curtailed. Most of Pertwee's first two series are set on present-day Earth, where the Time Lords have exiled the Doctor, disabling his TARDIS. At a time in the real world when inflation was raging and budgets were tightening, the BBC were keen to reduce the extra cost of designing completely new sets and costumes for every single story. The change also enabled a wider circle of regular characters to be established, creating a stronger team in front of the cameras. Either way, Pertwee's dandy Doctor with his love of cars, gadgets and a need for speed, was a hit with the fans. In 1975, a year after he had handed over the TARDIS keys to Tom Baker, one newspaper was still describing his as 'the longest running and most popular Doctor Who of them all'.[12]

But in time, Pertwee was to be eclipsed by his successor, whose bohemian mess of curly hair, wide-brimmed floppy hat and excessively long scarf remains many people's first thought whenever the Doctor is mentioned.[13] Baker had played a number of small television roles, as well as much film and theatre work, but was the least well-known actor to be cast in the role to date. Baker has often been described as being just as eccentric as the Doctor, and was a former monk who was working on a building site (between acting jobs) when offered his big TV break.

Baker's Doctor took a while to win over some viewers, with newspaper articles questioning whether he was making the Doctor too silly. Baker's response was that he 'was trying to stress his strangeness, that he is not of this world, not human, therefore his reactions would be different from ours'.[14] Arguably, Baker gave us the most alien Doctor of the classic series, yet also showed a deeper affinity with humans, whom he describes in 'The Ark In Space' (1975) as 'indomitable' and 'quite my favourite species'. Baker's era also represented the darkest period thematically in the show's history. Producer Phillip Hinchcliffe and script editor Robert Holmes worked together from 1975 to 1977, and deliberately gave many of their stories an air of gothic horror, drawing on source material such as Jekyll and Hyde ('Planet of Evil', 1975) and Frankenstein's monster ('The Brain of Morbius', 1976). Baker was enthusiastic about this aspect of the show, arguing that children loved to be terrorised in this way: scared, but safe in the knowledge that it wasn't real and that their family was watching with them. The fact that *Doctor Who* was genuine family viewing enabled it to go the extra mile in terror.

The Fall from Grace

Baker's seven-year stint in the TARDIS cast a shadow from which all of his 1980s successors struggled to escape. Certainly, the show enjoyed its biggest viewing figures during his time, and arguably this reflects it hitting a peak in terms of the quality of the stories during this period.

When Tom Baker finally left in 1981, the producers again looked for a marked contrast to what had gone before. Peter Davison was well known to TV viewers for his portrayal of young vet Tristan Farnham in the drama *All Creatures Great and Small*. Davison's Doctor was less extroverted than Baker's eccentric loon, and he showed more vulnerability than any of his predecessors. Davison's Doctor is often judged harshly in comparison to his madcap predecessor, with some pointing to his era as the beginning of the decline of *Doctor Who*. Nevertheless, despite a shaky start, by the time Davison left the role, he had won round most critics and the audience figures were on the up. The show's producer John Nathan-Turner felt that if Davison had been willing to stay for one more season, he would have secured a place as one of the best Doctors in the show's history. But that was not to be.

Davison acted on advice given by Patrick Troughton and only stayed for three years, departing in 1984. His replacement, Colin Baker, gave us the loudest, most arrogant Doctor to date. Justin Richards describes Baker's Doctor as having the same mood swings and changes in attitude as his predecessors, but in much more extreme fashion:

> Where the second Doctor might let slip an apt quote, the sixth will proclaim it. Where the third might take it for

granted that he is more intelligent than anyone else he meets, the sixth makes sure that they know it. Where the fourth might rail against injustice and evil, the sixth gives an almost operatic performance to make the point. If the first Doctor is acerbic, the sixth is positively caustic. And where the fifth Doctor is quietly passionate, the sixth Doctor has the same depth of feeling but at a considerably higher volume.[15]

Viewers were confused by the new Doctor. Colin Baker has since explained the character arc that was planned for the Doctor over the length of his four year contract. His initial persona – irritable, bombastic and confrontational – was to be gradually softened over time. However, time (ironically for *Doctor Who*) was the one thing that he never had. There was an 18-month gap between the end of his first full season and the beginning of his second. Apparently concerned about the levels of violence in the programme, BBC management put the show on hold for a year in order to have a major rethink of the format. Michael Grade, then in charge of BBC Drama, even publicly criticised the production team, calling them complacent and describing the show as having lost its imagination.

When the show did return, in September 1986, it was for a 14-week run, entitled 'Trial of a Time Lord'. This was the shortest in the history of the old series (although one week longer than the 2005 version) and ironically came at a time when the Doctor's television future was itself very much on trial. Towards the end of the run, Michael Grade told John Nathan-Turner that the show could return for a further series in 1987 on one condition: that Baker be replaced with a new Doctor.

That Doctor was Sylvester McCoy, a one-time trainee priest best known for his work on children's shows

Jigsaw and *Eureka*, and with a theatrical past that included working as a daredevil in *The Ken Campbell Roadshow*, igniting his own head and putting ferrets down his trousers. McCoy's Doctor represented a deliberate attempt to reintroduce some of the mystery that had originally surrounded the character. Over the years more and more of the blanks in the Doctor's background had been filled in. We knew who he was and where he came from in a way that had not been the original intention (it is easy to forget that we didn't even discover that he was a Time Lord until the end of the sixth series). Restoring the lost mystery was an important aspect of the attempt to revive the under-pressure show.

McCoy's Doctor resembles Troughton's more than any of his other predecessors, with his manipulation of people and events, and his deceptive habit of apparently not knowing what is going on. McCoy's is also the Doctor who most sharply divides opinion among fans. His best moments are generally those where he expresses his simmering rage against injustice and wrongdoing, rather than when he engages in comic business and pulling faces for the camera. For some, his era is the fag-end of a period of steady decline; for others, a renaissance which turned around a failing format and was cut down just as it was re-establishing itself. At its best, as in the impressive 'Remembrance of the Daleks' (1988), it holds its head up with the best of the golden years. At its worst, it shows everything that can go wrong for an under-resourced television show between page and screen. Andrew Cartmel was the script editor for the show during that period, and he recalls how 'Remembrance of the Daleks' writer Ben Aaronovitch couldn't even bring himself to watch what was done with another of his stories, the Arthurian-themed 'Battlefield' (1989):

I borrowed Ben's VHS tape of the story. When I put it into my machine, the tape was wound a few minutes into the first episode. 'Did you see where the tape was wound to?' says Ben. 'That was as far as I got. That was as much as I could bear to watch.'[16]

It seems that the viewers shared Aaronovitch's dis-appointment – 'Battlefield's' four episodes provided the lowest ever average viewing figures of any *Doctor Who* adventure. The commissioning of a further series, which would have been the 27th in the show's history, was put on hold. Although at the time they stopped short of actually announcing the death of *Doctor Who*, nobody in authority at the BBC seemed particularly keen to save it.

Russell T. Davies was a self-proclaimed fan who watched the show from childhood and stayed loyal to it to the very end of McCoy's era: 'I think it simply got old and a bit neglected, in the way that we all do. Can I say, I'm 40 now. I don't dress as well as I used to, I don't cut my hair as often as I should, and I'm a little bit rambling and eccentric and that happens to all of us, and I think that happened to the programme.'[17]

American Tragedy

In the mid-1990s, rumours emerged that Steven Spielberg's Amblin Entertainment were interested in acquiring the rights to *Doctor Who*, with a view to making a big-budget series aimed at the American market. The Amblin link never materialised, but in 1996 a TV movie version was made. Set in San Francisco on New Year's Eve 1999, it was clearly intended to sell the franchise in the States.

Sylvester McCoy made a brief return, to regenerate into the eighth Doctor, Paul McGann. The budget was bigger than anything previously seen in *Doctor Who*, but much of the essence of the show had been jettisoned. There were many brief nods to the old show – jelly babies, a yoyo, a multi-coloured scarf – but also a fundamental lack of understanding about how classic *Doctor Who* worked. *Who* stories usually present the Doctor with a puzzle, which gradually reveals itself – with the presence of Daleks, Cybermen or other recurring foes often kept secret until two or three episodes in. By contrast, the 1996 version can't even be bothered to get past the opening credits before revealing that the Doctor's old enemy, a rogue Time Lord known as the Master, is the cause of all that will follow.

There are some nice touches – the Doctor grabbing a traffic policeman's gun and threatening to shoot *himself* unless he is allowed to go free – but in truth, McGann's Doctor seems a pale imitation of his former selves, the plot is weak and despite the impressive visual spectacle of the inside of the TARDIS, the magic of the format got lost somewhere over the Atlantic. In comparison with the 2005 version, *Doctor Who: The Movie* seems to be a master class in how not to revive a once-great franchise. In any event, it failed to stimulate interest in an American series, and *Doctor Who* was left in limbo until Russell T. Davies came along seven years later.

Whose Who?

The lengthy gap enabled Christopher Eccleston to start with something of a clean slate, although his Doctor has shown something of the manic alien quality of Tom Baker, the playfulness of McCoy and Troughton, the vulnerability of Davison and the arrogance that has never been too far from the surface of all of the Doctors. While we wait with interest to see what his successor (and long time *Doctor Who* fan) David Tennant brings to the role, nobody seems too worried about whether the show can survive with a new leading man. In that regard, Tennant's situation is possibly closer to Pertwee's than to Troughton's. Christopher Eccleston has already established that the Doctor can be successfully brought up to date, and a third series has already been commissioned, even before the second one was written. Most importantly, the show has succeeded in winning back a broad, family audience.

Andrew Cartmel describes being interviewed by Jonathan Powell, then Head of Drama at the BBC, for the job of *Doctor Who* script editor:

> Finally Powell asked me, 'Who do you think *Doctor Who* is for?' I gave a politician's answer: '*Doctor Who* is for everyone.' Jonathan shook his head vigorously and contradicted me. '*Doctor Who* is for children,' he said very firmly.[18]

The 2005 version works hard to appeal to the children in the audience, with Slitheen fart gags, Mickey being swallowed by a wheelie-bin, and even an appearance by *Blue Peter* presenter Matt Baker. But the new show also caters for older, more sophisticated tastes. 'Father's Day' offers possibly the most emotionally powerful *Doctor Who* episode ever; 'Dalek' offers a profound examination of purpose and meaning; while the two parts of 'The Empty Child' and 'The Doctor Dances' are as chilling as anything from the horror-tinged stories of Tom Baker's heyday. Cartmel continues the account of his interview:

I said that I agreed, but I was lying through my teeth. I already believed with equal firmness, that it was an adult show with adult possibilities. Kids should be able to watch it and enjoy it too, preferably from behind the sofa, but we weren't catering to them. It had to be as intelligent and serious as any piece of adult drama.

It had to be *good*.[19]

Everyone involved in the 2005 show would agree. Quality was the benchmark of the new *Doctor Who*. Scripts, actors, budget and special effects, everything had to be just right. Russell T. Davies described 'simply making it good' as 'the biggest challenge in bringing *Doctor Who* back'.[20] The degree to which they have succeeded can be seen by the fact Michael Grade, now Chairman of the BBC and seen by many fans as 'the man who killed *Doctor Who*', wrote to Director General Mark Thompson congratulating all concerned for producing 'a classy, popular triumph for people of all ages and all backgrounds – real value for money for our license fee payers'.[21] The Doctor's most dangerous enemy had changed sides.

The desire to achieve something of this quality was a decisive factor in attracting Christopher Eccleston to the project:

I liked the idea of a writer as intelligent and rigorous as Russell writing for children, because I think if you can get them young with good stuff, as they grow older they're going to demand good stuff of their television.[22]

So there we have it: *Doctor Who* is once again a force for moral good. Sydney Newman's vision of an educational show has, in a sense, finally reasserted itself. Not content with saving the world, the Doctor was going to set about saving the standards of British television for future generations. If *Doctor Who* was going to find its new audience – young and old, male and female, long-standing *Who* fans and complete newcomers, then it had to be good. It was.

Notes

[1] Russell T. Davies, *Project Who* (BBC Audiobooks, 2005).

[2] Mal Young, *Project Who*.

[3] The name is an acronym for 'Time And Relative Dimensions In Space'. It tells you much about the nature of science fiction fandom that there is heated debate about whether or not there should be an 's' on the end of 'Dimension'.

[4] Russell T. Davies, in Nick Griffiths, 'They're back . . . and this time it's war!' *Radio Times*, 18–25 June 2005, p. 15.

[5] Russell T. Davies, *SFX* magazine, July 2005, p. 46.

[6] Terrance Dicks, *The Story of Doctor Who* (BBC2, first broadcast as part of '*Doctor Who* Night', Saturday 19 March 2005).

[7] Russell T. Davies, *Radio Times* 18–25 June 2005, p. 15.

[8] Will Cohen, *Doctor Who Confidential: The Good, the Bad and the Ugly* (BBC3, first broadcast 2 April 2005).

[9] Peter Haining, *Doctor Who A Celebration: Two Decades Through Time and Space* (Virgin 1995. First published by W.H. Allen & Co, 1983), p. 13.

[10] Russell T. Davies, in Benjamin Cook, 'A Long Game', *Doctor Who Magazine*, 17 August 2005, p. 36.

[11] Adrian Rigelsford, *The Doctors: 30 years of Time Travel* (Boxtree, 1994) p. 57. Rigelsford has been criticised for allegedly inventing quotes from fictitious interviews when the subject is no longer alive for corroboration, most notably regarding Rigelsford's claims to have conducted the last ever interview with film director Stanley Kubrick. However, this report of Newman's comment was published three years before the latter's death, and we reproduce it here in good faith.

[12] Chris Kenworthy, 'Does Doctor Who's TARDIS need an MOT test?' Article reproduced on www.cuttingsarchive. org.uk/news_mag/1970s/cuttings/unk221175-mot.htm, and credited to 'unknown newspaper, 22 November 1975.'

[13] The fourth Doctor's costume was inspired by a painting of French artist Tolouse Lautrec, but the now legendary scarf was a happy accident – the result of a freelance knitter not realising she didn't have to use all the wool she had been given. cf. 'The History of Tom Baker's Scarves' at www. geocities.com/Area51/Zone/3746/Scarf.html.

[14] 'Never mind the Daleks, can Dr Who survive the biggest threat yet to his existence?' *Daily Mail* 1975, reproduced on www.cuttingsarchive.org.uk/news_mag/1970s/cuttings/ mail1975-survive.htm.

[15] Justin Richards, *Doctor Who The Legend: 40 Years of Time Travel* (BBC Books, 2003), p. 327.

[16] Andrew Cartmel, *Script Doctor: The Inside Story of Doctor Who 1986–1989.* (Reynolds and Hearn, 2005), p.150.

[17] Russell T. Davies, *Project Who.*

[18] Andrew Cartmel, *Script Doctor*, p. 13.

[19] Andrew Cartmel, *Script Doctor*, p. 14.

[20] Russell T. Davies, *Project Who.*

[21] Michael Grade, www.bbc.co.uk/cult/news/drwho/2005/ 06/21/20120.shtml.

[22] Christopher Eccleston, *Doctor Who Confidential: Bringing Back the Doctor* (BBC3, first broadcast 26 March 2005).

2. Time's Hero

**'But after all these revelations, there is one
mystery you still haven't explained.
Answer me this: who are you?'
'Just a friend, passing through.'**
*Charles Dickens and the Doctor in
'The Unquiet Dead'*

A young shop assistant backs warily away from a threatening throng of living shop dummies. The department store wall halts her retreat. She does *not* scream. The blank-eyed plastic mannequins raise their arms to seal her fate. Suddenly, someone takes hold of her hand, pulling her to safety. Our heroine (and a new generation of viewers) has met our hero, and life will never be the same: 'I'm the Doctor, by the way,' the stranger informs her a few moments later, 'what's your name?' 'Rose', she replies. 'Nice to meet you Rose,' says the Doctor, 'Run for your life!'

Hero

Saving a shop assistant from a crowd of Autons is the essence of *Doctor Who*, both the TV programme and the character. The Doctor is a hero. Christopher Eccleston describes him as:

> Pragmatic, witty, brave, intelligent, anarchic, heroic and
> caring – he cares about life in all its forms, and has a
> permanent sense of wonder at the world and everything
> in it. He's also childlike, contradictory, brutal to his
> enemies, and constantly restless and inquisitive.[1]

Eccleston aimed to portray the Doctor as an 'idealistic,
humane alien' with a 'melancholy side' that comes from
the loneliness of being 'an outsider'.[2] As Terrance Dicks,
observed: 'The Doctor believes in good and fights evil.
Though often caught up in violent situations, he is a
man of peace. He is never cruel or cowardly. In fact, to
put it simply, the Doctor is a hero.'[3]

We see this heroism when the Doctor leaps between
the whirling blades of Platform One to reactivate the
space station forcefields; when he stands in the way of
an oncoming Reaper in 'Father's Day'; and when he
declares his intention to rescue Rose after the Daleks
have ordered him to stay out of their way at the end
of 'Bad Wolf'. The essence of the Doctor is to stand up
for the sake of others, even if doing so puts his own
life in danger.

The Doctor is a unique hero because he combines
an otherworldly, alien intellect with a quintessentially
British eccentricity. Even in *Doctor Who*: *The Movie*
(1996), co-produced by the BBC and America's
Universal Pictures, Paul McGann's Doctor remained
recognisably British. The Doctor takes his place among
iconic characters of British fiction such as James Bond
and Sherlock Homes, despite not coming from Britain
– or indeed planet Earth – at all.

Where other conventional heroes are quick to fight
their way out of trouble, the Doctor prefers to use his
brain rather than his brawn. Where *Star Trek*'s Captain
Kirk barrelled around the universe with a phaser and

a bank of photon torpedoes, the Doctor makes do with a sonic screwdriver. Although the character has become more physically vigorous since his first incarnation, violence has always been regarded as the weapon of last resort. Christopher Eccleston's Doctor may pick up a gun with the enthusiastic exclamation 'lock and load' ('Dalek'), but he also concedes that he was never going to fire at the staff of Bad Wolf TV. The Doctor is so opposed to violence that he even admits to having destroyed a factory producing sonic guns and replacing it with a banana plantation (because 'bananas are good').

Traditionally, the Doctor has differed from other models of the hero by not becoming romantically engaged with the characters he meets along the way. Ironically, given Cassandra's put-down in 'The End of the World' ('I bet you were the school swot and never got kissed'), the 2005 version sees the Doctor become much more flirtatious than any of his predecessors. Where in the past the show played down any sense of romance (let alone anything more) involving the Doctor, Eccleston playfully flirts with Jabe in 'The End of the World', with Lynda in 'Bad Wolf' and even with Captain Jack. But his relationship with Rose lies at the heart of the 2005 show, and despite her repeated claims that they are not a couple, it is certainly the case that the emotional bond between the two is of a different order to any previous Doctor/companion relationship. Although the kiss they share in 'Parting of the Ways' is a necessary life-saving act, it is clear that it is also more than just that.

Alien

The Doctor is an alien, as he makes clear to Rose when she first enters the TARDIS. In fact, he is a Time Lord from the planet Gallifrey. There are a number of ways in which his non-human nature is demonstrated, most dramatically in his ability to cheat death by regenerating into a completely new form when one of his bodies dies. He explains something of this to Rose, before transforming into David Tennant, and then carrying on his conversation about the planet Barcelona. Christopher Eccleston recalls that as a child he was: 'fascinated by the idea of someone being the same person on the inside, but suddenly looking different on the outside.'4 Although Eccleston was denied a scene where the previous Doctor regenerates into him, he was given the traditional new Doctor post-regeneration mirror scene: at Rose's house in 'Rose' he peers into a mirror and says: 'Uh; could have been worse. But look at the ears!'5

The Doctor has passive telepathic skills linked to his TARDIS, which may explain why he gains many people's trust so quickly. Sylvester McCoy's Doctor even borrowed *Star Wars'* Jedi mind trick on more than one occasion. The TARDIS's telepathy is also used as an explanation for the ability of companions to understand alien languages. This also underlines the Doctor's alien-ness, as he takes for granted something that seems utterly strange to Rose, who is far from amused when she discovers that the TARDIS has been messing around with the inside of her head. Little did she realise just how extreme her own relationship with the TARDIS was to become.

Over the various series of *Doctor Who*, a number of other details about his physiology have emerged: The Doctor has two hearts, together with an inhuman blood type (thicker than human blood). The Doctor can go into a trance that limits his need for oxygen and can withstand the absolute cold of space for six minutes or so. He is also allergic to certain gases (or at least was in his fifth incarnation – in the final adventure of Peter Davison's Doctor, he finally explained the stick of celery that had been carried on his lapel for three years as being an early warning strategy).

The Doctor's age has ranged between 450 and 953 over the years of the show, with the trend for it to slowly and consistently creep upwards. In the 2005 series, Eccleston's Doctor rounds this down to 900 when around Rose. Whether this is for convenience or out of male vanity is a debatable point.

Outsider

Doctor: It's never been easy being the only child left out in the cold.
Nancy: I suppose you'd know.
Doctor: I would actually.

('The Empty Child')

The Doctor is displaced. He has the air of a small boy locked out on a cold night, knowing that however much he presses his face to the window, he does not belong inside in the warm. This sense of rootlessness has always been part of the Doctor's psychological make-up, with William Hartnell's Doctor describing himself as 'a wanderer in the fourth dimension' and reflecting that 'sometimes I feel like I'd like to belong somewhere, not just be a wanderer' ('The Sensorites', 1964). This is echoed by Eccleston's Doctor who (not entirely convincingly) tells Lynda, 'I'm just a traveller wandering past. Believe it or not, all I'm after is a quiet life.'

Eccleston's Doctor takes on a new element of isolation as the last of the Time Lords. When Rose first questions

him about his background, he is defensive and hostile,
stating just that 'this is who I am, right here right now,
all right? All that counts is here and now, and this is
me' ('The End of the World'). Gradually he reveals more
information about his past, and in particular his part in
the Time War. But the sense of being cut adrift from
his roots, of being lost in space and time with no way
home, is central to Eccleston's portrayal of the Doctor.

What's in a Name?

The Doctor has always sought to keep his identity
hidden. Most of the time he is happy to leave it as 'just
the Doctor', but occasionally (as in 'The Empty Child')
he uses the pseudonym 'John Smith'. This name was
first used by the Doctor in 'The Wheel In Space' (1968),
where he takes it from a piece of medical equipment on-
board a space station, and it has appeared sporadically
in the show ever since.

We have a few hints that suggest the sort of name
the Doctor might have. 'Who' is used sparingly as the
Doctor's proper name. In 'The War Machines' (1966),
two characters refer to him as 'Doctor Who'. He adopts
the German alias of 'Dr Von Wer' in 'The Highlanders'
(1966/67), and signs himself 'Dr W' in 'The Underwater
Menace' (1967). Jon Pertwee's second story as the Doctor
was called 'Doctor Who and the Silurians' (1970).
Some have suggested that, like companion and fellow
Time Lord Romana (full name Romanadvoratrelundar),
the Doctor has abbreviated an unwieldy name which
begins with the syllable 'Who'. However, this is pure
speculation. While for a few years the writers seemed
to suggest that 'Who' was part of the Doctor's name,
for the majority of the show's history 'Who' has merely

been part of a question about his identity. What is clear is that the lack of a name helps to preserve the mystery of his character.

Doctor of What?

Over the centuries the Doctor has made various statements about his qualifications. In 'The Moonbase' (1967) he claims to have qualified for a doctorate in medicine under Joseph Lister in Glasgow in 1888 (although Lister left Glasgow some eleven years prior to this). On other occasions he denies being a doctor of medicine, and says that his degree was 'purely honorary' ('The Ark In Space', 1975). All of this, however, only concerns qualifications gained on Earth.

The Doctor obtained some sort of advanced qualification analogous to a human doctorate from Prydon Academy before leaving Gallifrey (although he only scraped a pass). In 'Revenge of the Cybermen' (1975) the Doctor refers to himself as a 'doctor of many things', so we can suppose that this may have been a combined doctorate. He is a scientist, an engineer, and an expert in Gallifreyan law. Once, in 'Time and the Rani' (1987), he laid claim to having 'a unique conceptual understanding of the properties of time.' But the Doctor's knowledge is less a matter of formal qualifications, and more to do with his insatiable curiosity. He is always asking questions, and he is at his most effusive in praising his associates for demonstrating an ability to question and to think for themselves.

Fantastic Curiosity

It is this relentless curiosity which drives the Doctor from adventure to adventure. In 'Aliens of London' he says, 'This is what I travel for, Rose, to see history happening right in front of us.' He is an enthusiastic amateur, fascinated by the universe and itching to explore and discover. Russell T. Davies praises the Doctor's amateur status: 'What I love about the Doctor is that he doesn't travel space and time because it's his job, he does it out of an inexhaustible sense of adventure.'[6] As we have already seen, the Doctor is more likely to get himself out of a sticky situation with the schoolboy contents of his pockets (yo-yo, cricket ball, jelly babies) and with his mind than with a gun. There is more than a little of Sherlock Holmes in the Doctor, with his fierce intellect by far his most potent weapon against the forces of evil. Indeed, the parallels between the two characters were made explicit in the Tom Baker adventure 'The Talons of Weng Chiang' (1977), which saw the Doctor sporting a Holmes-like deerstalker and cape while trying to solve mysterious murders in London's theatreland.

The Doctor's enthusiasm when faced with danger is another reflection of his 'gentleman amateur' tendencies. Most people wouldn't respond to the sight of a panic-struck theatre audience fleeing in terror with 'That's more like it!' but it is characteristic of the Doctor. The same tendency was given a more glamorous expression by Jon Pertwee's Doctor, with his love of cars, bikes, hovercraft and any other new-fangled vehicle that the producers thought would give them an exciting chase scene.

Technology is another of the Doctor's passions. When Captain Jack mocks him for making a sonic screwdriver (as opposed to, say, a sonic cannon or a sonic disruptor), the Doctor asks, 'What, have you never been bored? Never had a long night? Never had a lot of cabinets to put up?' ('The Doctor Dances').

The Doctor's homemade sonic screwdriver was introduced by Patrick Troughton's Doctor, lost by Peter Davison and re-introduced by Sylvester McCoy during his brief appearance in *Doctor Who: The Movie* (1996). It can unlock doors, de-activate Autons, re-attach barbed wire and even, in desperate circumstances, unscrew screws. The long absence of the sonic screwdriver was the result of a decision by John Nathan-Turner, producer of the show from 1979 to its 1989 demise. He felt that the device's multipurpose flexibility was too convenient, allowing an easy way out for the Doctor and his scriptwriters alike. When commissioning Eric Saward to write 'The Visitation' (1982), he gave him instructions to include a scene where the screwdriver was destroyed. Russell T. Davies has no such qualms about the sonic screwdriver, saying: 'so long as the sonic screwdriver never solves the plot in the end' it is 'just a faster way of story telling'.[7] Nevertheless, the sonic screwdriver can also be seen as the meeting point of several facets of the Doctor's personality, combining his opposition to violence, his creativity, his insatiable curiosity and his love of technology.

Alien Quixote

Our first introduction to the Doctor's roots came at the close of Troughton's last story, 'The War Games' (1969). When the Doctor is put on trial by his own race, previously unanswered questions about his origins were addressed. He was a Time Lord, from a race who had mastered time travel. But while other Time Lords were content to merely observe, the Doctor would always actively fight against evil wherever he found it, even if this brought him into conflict with his own people. The

Doctor was a rebel, but one whose rebellion was fired by his relentless curiosity and his unfailing sense of fair play, rather than the more Machiavellian tendencies of other rogue Time Lords who cropped up in the show from time to time.

The Doctor's willingness to challenge authority is not restricted to that of his own people. A common element in the Earth-bound adventures of the Pertwee era was the Doctor's efforts being impeded by small-minded governmental bureaucrats. When faced with worthy authority, such as the Guardian in 'Colony In Space' (1971) or the Draconian emperor in 'Frontier In Space' (1973), he is capable of showing appropriate deference and respect. But when authority figures do nothing to deserve respect, the Doctor will bristle indignantly and treat them with utter contempt.

Time Lords come from the planet Gallifrey, which is probably near the galactic core, and are the oldest galactic race. After acquiring the ability to travel in time and space, one of their first acts was an attempt to guide the development of the Minyan race, who subsequently treated the Time Lords as gods. This intervention proved to be so disastrous that the leaders of the Time Lords vowed never again to interfere in the affairs of other worlds. However, the Doctor rejects this attitude, arguing that the strong have a moral duty to protect the weak from evil. His own approach to the freedom of time travel is much less cautious, as he explains in 'The Long Game':

> The thing is, Adam, time travel is like visiting Paris: you can't just read the guidebook, you've got to throw yourself in – eat the food, use the wrong verbs, get charged double and end up kissing complete strangers. Or is that just me? Stop asking questions, go on and do it.

In 'Boom Town', Margaret Slitheen suggests that the Doctor's practice of reckless engagement is one that leaves him open to the accusation of dodging responsibility for his actions:

> I bet you're always the first to leave, Doctor. Never mind the consequences, off you go. You butchered my family then ran for the stars – am I right?

Although the Doctor states at the end of 'The Long Game' that he prefers to leave the clearing up to others, that doesn't mean that he ignores the moral difficulties of his interventionist approach. Ultimately, the Doctor interferes because somebody has to. In 'World War Three' he says, 'This is my life, Jackie. It's not fun, it's not smart, it's just standing up and making a decision because nobody else will.' Sometimes the Doctor makes mistakes – when he deals with the problem of a controlling news media in 'The Long Game', he just creates the conditions for a greater danger to humanity in 'Bad Wolf'. Nevertheless, the Doctor recognises the need for individuals to do what they can to change unjust situations wherever they find them.

Power Behind the Throne

Although the Doctor frequently found himself at odds with his own people, he is an important figure in Time Lord history. He once stood for election as President of the Time Lords ('The Deadly Assassin', 1976). The only other candidate turned out to be a stooge for the Master and died before the election, leaving the Doctor as President-elect by default. He left Gallifrey before he could be invested, but later returned to take up the Presidency ('The Invasion of Time', 1978). On a subsequent visit he was informed that his Presidency had lapsed due to continued absence from Gallifrey ('Trial of a Time Lord', 1986). In the McCoy era the scriptwriters seemed intent on according the Doctor even higher honour than this, hinting in 'Remembrance of the Daleks' (1988) that he worked alongside Omega and Rassilon, the original developers of Gallifreyan time travel technology and founding fathers of Time Lord society.

In the 2005 revival of the show, the Doctor is again 'more than just another Time Lord', as he is (apparently) the only Time Lord to survive the Time War. But don't be too surprised if in subsequent series we discover that other travellers from Gallifrey are still on the scene. History in *Doctor Who* is always open to rewriting, and as the Doctor himself is fond of saying, 'Time will tell. It always does.'

The Doctor's experience of life is very different from ours. In 'Rose', he describes being able to feel 'the ground beneath our feet ... spinning at 1000 miles an hour, and the entire planet ... hurtling around the sun at 67,000 miles an hour'. In 'Parting of the Ways', when Rose describes the effect of absorbing power from the TARDIS's time vortex, she says that she can 'see everything. All that is, all that was, all that ever could be', to which the Doctor replies that he sees that all the time. We don't know if this perception is common to all Time Lords, but the Doctor is undeniably a man of mystery and great power.

Secret Agent

Another aspect of the Doctor's life hinted at in the older versions of the show is his role as an official secret agent for the Time Lords. The Celestial Intervention Agency (or CIA), mentioned in 'The Deadly Assassin' (1976), are a secretive Time Lord group who may sometimes direct the Doctor's wanderings – a plausible explanation for how he 'just happens' to stumble across so many dangerous situations requiring his unique talents. According to the CIA theory, at the end of 'The War Games' (1969), the Doctor is not immediately exiled to Earth, but is secretly offered his freedom in return for undertaking missions for the CIA. In 'The Two Doctors' (1985), Patrick Troughton returns as the second Doctor, but is an older version of himself, with a TARDIS that has been modified in a number of ways since 'The War Games' (1969). Similarly, at the beginning of Jon Pertwee's first adventure 'Spearhead From Space' (1970), he is wearing a ring, a bracelet and a watch that homes in on the TARDIS. The Doctor had none of these gadgets at the end of the previous story. Some fans have pointed to these apparent 'errors' as evidence that the Doctor has had a number of further adventures between the end of 'The War Games' and the beginning of 'Spearhead From Space'. Of course, all of this could also be attributed to nothing more than the show's notorious disregard for continuity.

Saviour

To simply say that the Doctor is a hero does not do justice to the mythic quality of his character. According to Lou Anders:

> Doctor Who is the truest expression of Joseph Campbell's *Hero With a Thousand Faces* ever conceived. The idea of an alien, come down to earth, repeatedly dying and

resurrecting for the salvation of others is as close to the perpetual re-enactment of the eternal Hero's Journey as you can hope to find.[8]

This description of the Doctor as a figure who comes down to earth to die for others before being resurrected draws a clear analogy with Christian beliefs about Jesus. Describing *Doctor Who*, Sylvester McCoy explicitly draws this parallel:

It's the classic tale of the little man against great odds. That, and the other classic story of someone from outside our world coming down to help us. That makes it very attractive to human beings. I don't mean to be sacrilegious, but Jesus came down from outside the world to save us and it's that kind of arena.[9]

The parallels with Jesus are most deliberately played out in *Doctor Who: The Movie*, where Paul McGann appears wrapped, shroud-like, in a hospital sheet and is mistaken by a porter for the returning Jesus. Later the Master puts a device on the Doctor's head which bears an unmistakable resemblance to a crown of thorns. There are a number of other parallels in *Doctor Who* generally that can be observed when comparing the Doctor with Jesus:

(1) The Doctor is an unearthly figure who has a human form.
(2) He turns up out of the blue at just the right time and place to make a crucial difference, as if directed by providence or a higher power.
(3) He is motivated by a strong sense of good and evil, of the way things should and should not be: 'I can't stand burnt toast, I loathe bus stations.

Terrible places, full of lost luggage and lost souls and then there's unrequited love, and tyranny, and cruelty' ('Ghost Light', 1989).

(4) He has miraculous powers, including knowledge about the future, the power to heal the sick and to defeat demons.

(5) His archenemy, the Master, with his goatee beard and widow's peak hairline, has strong associations with classic representations of the Devil. In 'The Mark of the Rani' (1985) the Doctor even refers to the Master as: 'the prince of darkness'.

(6) The Doctor has 'disciples', companions who travel with him and support his mission (even though they often fail to understand what he is doing until hindsight reveals all).

(7) The Doctor is often viewed with suspicion by those he tries to help, and accused of crimes he has not committed (murder, being a spy, etc.). He is persecuted and threatened with death because he upsets the status quo.

(8) He is put on trial by his own people.

(9) Whenever possible, he tries to achieve his goal by making a reasoned, ethical appeal to those who will listen.

(10) He resorts to force only when the absolute evil of his opposition means that a peaceful approach has no hope of success. The only recorded instance of Jesus resorting to physical force is when he drove money-changers out of the temple courtyard in Jerusalem.[10]

(11) He sacrifices his own life in order to save people from evil. The Doctor does this on several occasions – in 'The Parting of the Ways', he does so to save Rose from the heart of the TARDIS. In 'The Caves of Androzani' (1984) he sacrificed his life to save Peri, whom he had only recently met.

(12) However, out of his death comes new life – not just for those he saves, but also for himself, as he is resurrected from the dead with a new body.

(13) When he returns from the dead even his closest friends can be sceptical that it really is him, until his characteristic behaviour convinces them that it is.

(14) After his work is done, he leaves the world, miraculously transcending it.

(15) He promises to return at an unspecified date in the future. The first Doctor left his granddaughter Susan behind on a post Dalek-invasion earth; his promise to return 'one day' was fulfilled at the close of 'The Five Doctors' (1983).

Survivor

Doctor Who has survived for over four decades (on and off screen) because he is a fantastic icon of a British ideal of heroism. With his 2005 television revival came an additional back-story of survival that cleverly introduced his alien roots to a new audience and added a dark new layer of psychology to the character.

Throughout the 2005 season it was gradually revealed that the Doctor is the last surviving member of his race, who were destroyed in a galaxy-spanning Time War with the Daleks. 'Dalek' revealed the fact that the Doctor himself brought the Time War to an end: 'I saw it happen, I made it happen!' On BBC3's *Doctor Who Confidential*, Christopher Eccleston commented that the Daleks were the Doctor's equivalent of Superman's Kryptonite, and that they were the one alien race that really scared him: 'He's a darker Doctor, because he's frightened.'[11] According to Russell T. Davies: 'That is the Doctor's survival guilt coming out ... That's a man who now strides through the universe wearing a tough leather jacket saying "don't touch me" ... who doesn't want a companion at first, who's quite reluctant until he gets to like her.'[12] The Doctor gradually changes over the course of the season: 'Going through episode six and facing the Dalek is a bit of therapy. There are better ways of therapy I'm sure, but ... nonetheless he fought a Dalek and he's a bit better after episode six. It's like, you've let go of the past a little bit, starts to re-build himself and become a new man.'[13]

In particular, his relationship with Rose seems to have been just the medicine the Doctor ordered. Their relationship gradually helps him to make peace with himself. It helps him to re-discover his moral centre as someone who defends the weak and the oppressed, even if it means sacrificing one of his lives; not out of guilt for the past (which arguably influences his judgement and behaviour in 'The Unquiet Dead'), or fear of his enemies (which undeniably has an effect in 'Dalek'), but out of love ('Parting of the Ways'):

> Finally, he's put in a position again where, instead of giving your life for Time Lords and Daleks and great big mythological concepts that are very much off-stage, it's for Rose; it's for that 19-year-old shop girl from planet Earth who is braver than brave and more loyal than anyone else in the universe; she is dying, and he gives his life for her. Never mind wars, never mind epic mythology, never mind all that grandstand stuff; it's absolutely personal, and he's at his most human. Right at the end he does a very, very human thing, and gives his life.[14]

No man is an island, even a mythic, alien hero with thirteen lives.

Notes

[1] Christopher Eccleston, *Radio Times Doctor Who Collector's Special*, (*Radio Times*, 26 March–1 April, 2005), p. 3.

[2] Christopher Eccleston, 'Time for a change, says new Dr Who', *Daily Telegraph*, Thursday 29 April, 2005.

[3] Terrance Dicks, quoted by Paul Cornell, Martin Day & Keith Topping, *Classic British TV*, (Guiness, 1996), p. 298.

[4] Christopher Eccleston, *Radio Times Doctor Who Collector's Special*, p. 3.

[5] This implies that when we meet the Doctor in 'Rose' he is newly regenerated. However, Clive shows Rose pictures of Eccleston's Doctor in various apparently solo travels which are difficult to fit into the span of the Doctor's life covered by the 2005 series. One possibility is that the Doctor did all these things in between his two invitations to Rose to join him at the end of 'Rose'.

[6] Russell T. Davies, *Radio Times Doctor Who Collector's Special*, p. 2.

[7] Russell T. Davies, *Doctor Who Confidential: Weird Science* (BBC3, first broadcast 28 May 2005).

[8] Lou Anders, in Cornell, Day & Topping, *The Discontinuity Guide*, (MonkeyBrain Books, 2004), p. 10.

[9] Sylvester McCoy, interview in *The Reading Chronicle*, quoted in *Doctor Who Magazine*, 25 June 2003.

[10] The significance of this action is that the courtyard was the only part of the temple area where foreigners were allowed to worship. By turning it into a place of commerce, the money-changers were preventing gentile believers from worshipping God. See Mt. 21:12–17.

[11] Christopher Eccleston, *Doctor Who Confidential: The Daleks* (BBC3, first broadcast 30 April 2005).

[12] Russell T. Davies, *Doctor Who Confidential: The Last Battle* (BBC3, first broadcast 18 June 2005).

[13] Russell T. Davies, *Doctor Who Confidential: The Last Battle*.

[14] Russell T. Davies, *Doctor Who Confidential: The Last Battle*.

3. I Only Take The Best

**One day, just one day maybe,
I'm going to meet someone who gets the whole
'don't wander off' thing.**

The Doctor in 'The Empty Child'

Our TV screens show a shot of the moon. The camera pans round to show a close up of a corner of the Earth. We rapidly zoom in to Britain, London, a house, a girl. The montage that follows takes us through a day in Rose Tyler's life and introduces us to the character who will be our eyes and ears in the Doctor's travels for the next 13 weeks and several billion years.

It's worth noting that the 2005 series of *Doctor Who* doesn't start with a sinister alien presence plotting the destruction of life on Earth, and it doesn't start with the Doctor arriving somewhere and trying to work out what is going on. It starts with Rose. More than that, it starts with Rose's ordinary life – it is a full three minutes before we get our first glimpse of something out of the ordinary, as Rose follows a mysterious noise in the basement of Hendrik's, the department store where she works.

By taking us through Rose's life before the Doctor, we get a sense of why she eventually agrees to travel with him. Rose's life was nothing special – 'no A levels, no job, no future' is how she sums it up (admittedly, the 'no job' part is a direct result of the Doctor blowing up her place of employment). She doesn't seem too concerned about her lack of direction when we first meet her – she is seen laughing and joking with Mickey during a lunch break – but it is nevertheless clear that something was missing.

Noel Clarke, who plays Mickey, sums up Rose's moment of decision as being clinched by the realisation that 'there's more to life than sitting on the couch watching her boyfriend watch football.'[1] As we discover in countless episodes during the course of the series, Rose is brave and adventurous, intelligent and always asking the right questions. Having had a glimpse of the kind of life the Doctor offered, it was inevitable that she would be unable to settle for the mundane alternative.

Chips With Everything

Rose's exposure to the Doctor's life has a profound effect upon her. In 'Rose' when the Doctor dismisses humanity, saying that all they do is 'eat chips, go to bed and watch telly', it is clear that the description applies equally to Rose. By the time the Doctor sends her home in 'Parting of the Ways', things have changed to the extent that there is an echo of the Doctor's words in her comment to Jackie:

> What do I do every day, Mum? What do I do? Get up, catch the bus, go to work, come back home, eat chips and go to bed. Is that it?

Life with the Doctor has changed Rose forever, not only bringing out a side of her personality that she may not have realised was there, but also exposing her to possibilities that she had never considered. Like Charles Dickens in 'The Unquiet Dead', Rose has just realised that there is more to learn.

The scene in a café that Rose shares with Mickey and Jackie in 'Parting of the Ways' reveals how much she has grown up over the previous 13 episodes. As she despairs at returning to her old life she comments:

> It was a better life. I don't mean all the travelling, and seeing aliens and spaceships and things – that don't matter. The Doctor showed me a better way of living your life. [To Mickey] You know, he showed you too. You don't just give up, you don't just let things happen. You make a stand, you say 'no', you've the guts to do what's right when everyone else runs away.

Life with the Doctor has taught Rose to take responsibility and do the right thing.

Old Friends

Russell T. Davies says that the companion 'is your way in to the story ... your point of view'[2] and it is true that one of the important roles played by companions in *Doctor Who* is as a basic aid to storytelling. The companion exists so that the Doctor has someone to explain everything to, someone who asks the questions that enable the audience to know what is going on. Two exceptions to this have been the robot dog K9 (1977–1981), and the shape-changing robot Kamelion (1983–1984), who each served primarily as plot devices to get the Doctor in and out of trouble. It is noticeable that throughout the history of the show, the Doctor almost never travels alone. Tom Baker had a companionless gap of just one story ('The Deadly Assassin', 1976) where he both arrives and departs alone, but even then he finds allies who aid him in his struggle with the Master. Other than that solitary experience, the Doctor has always either arrived with company, or taken somebody new away with him at the end of each adventure. The Doctor may be perfectly able to fight evil single-handed, but it wouldn't make such good television.

In addition to being the audience's eyes and ears, *Doctor Who* companions have traditionally filled a number of other roles. The majority have been female, and even the longest running male companions have never remained without female company in the TARDIS for any length of time. The show's producers have clearly worked hard at providing variety between the many women in the Doctor's life. They have been brainy like Zoë (1968–69), Liz (1970), Nyssa (1981–1983) and fellow Time Lord Romana (1978–1979 and 1979–1981); scatty like Jo (1971–1973); brave like Leela (1977–1978) and Ace (1987–1989); timid like Victoria (1967–1968) and reluctant like Tegan (1981–1984). The one thing they have all had in common is the ability to scream.

The stereotype of the screaming, helpless female is part of the cultural baggage that *Doctor Who* has carried with it through the years. Peter Davison has commented that he 'always thought that the role of the side-kick was exactly to say, "Help me Doctor"',[3] and most of them did so at the top of their lungs. Although attempts were made to make the companions more acceptable to the growing women's liberation movement in the 1970s, such moves probably represented mere lip service to the idea of an independent woman, and the pattern of the clever Doctor coming to the rescue of his helpless side-kick was repeated again and again.

More disturbing for the feminists was the use of the female companions as eye candy to keep dads watching the show. Even strong female companions like Leela suffer this indignity. The price of gaining a fearless female warrior from a primitive tribe, was an animal skin costume that showed more of Leela's skin than that of the luckless animals who provided the pelts. Peter Davison's regeneration scene in 1984 suggests that the producers knew exactly what they were doing in this regard, with companion Peri crouching down over the Doctor and facing square-on to the camera. Davison has commented that for all his 'is this death?' emoting, the thing that everyone remembers about the scene is Nicola Bryant's cleavage. Janet Fielding, who played Tegan, recounts how producer John Nathan-Turner had even told her that she was 'there for the dads'.[4] When she finally managed to escape the infamous 'boob tube' costume that was forced on her for five whole adventures, she asked if it could be burned.

Rough and Ready

The male companions in *Doctor Who* have always taken on the task of tackling action scenes that the Doctor is unable to handle himself. The relative frailness of William Hartnell's Doctor meant that if there was any fighting to be done, they needed a younger man about the place. Hartnell had a succession of heavies, while Patrick Troughton was accompanied from his second story to the bitter end by Jamie, (who also rejoined the series with him in 1985 for 'The Two Doctors').

The presence of such burly side-kicks enabled the programme-makers to eat their cake and have it: they could make the Doctor a man of peace and still make fight scenes an integral part of the format. The view has often been expressed that the Doctor should never wield a gun (although on occasions, he has turned to them as a last resort), but there is no such problem with putting a weapon in the hands of his more hot-headed fellow-travellers.

The arrival of a more dynamic Doctor in the person of Jon Pertwee, along with the permanent presence of UNIT soldiers under the authority of Brigadier Lethbridge-Stewart, meant that there was less need for a regular male character to accompany the Doctor wherever he went. As a result, the show entered an era of coupling the Doctor with a succession of solitary females. Liz, Jo, Sarah-Jane, Leela and two different Romanas came and went, (with UNIT medical officer Harry Sullivan tagging along for a few adventures at the beginning of Tom Baker's era) before Adric stowed aboard at the end of 'Full Circle' (1980). By the time Baker handed the TARDIS over to Peter Davison, it was as full as ever before, with Romana and K9 gone but with Adric joined by Nyssa and Tegan.

Barefoot in the TARDIS

Janet Fielding has complained about *Doctor Who*'s one-dimensional treatment of female companions in general, and her character in particular: 'It settled down to a sort of action series when I was doing it, and so there was very little in terms of character or anything like that ... Character and personality are not the same thing. Tegan was a personality, you know, the kind of slightly grumpy, brash Australian ... that's not a character.'[5] Fielding goes on to comment that the very structure of the show makes it harder for women to receive a good dramatic treatment:

I don't know that the male companions fared that badly. Okay, so you need somebody in the TARDIS who doesn't know so much so that they can ask questions in order to get over exposition . . . I just think it's less acceptable to find women in that role.

As Fielding observes, the problem with providing the Doctor with capable, intelligent help – male or female – is that it undermines the suitability of the character as the audience's point of view. Not that all *Doctor Who* fans are stupid, or that we can only identify with feeble, helpless characters, but if the Doctor is accompanied by an accomplished scientist, there is no reason why the Doctor needs to explain things in layman's terms. Jon Pertwee's original assistant Liz Shaw was replaced by the more muddle-headed charms of Jo Grant precisely because of the writers' frustration at the narrative problems caused by her scientific expertise.

However, as society's view of a 'woman's role' began to change, so *Doctor Who* began to include female companions who were as inclined to action as any of the men. The most obvious example is Leela, who was always ready to draw her knife and leap into battle whenever the situation called for it (and often when it didn't, according to the Doctor). Tom Baker was reportedly unhappy about having such a bloodthirsty assistant, feeling that the Doctor would be unlikely to tolerate such behaviour. Something of this disapproval possibly spills over into the many scenes where the Doctor upbraids Leela for her latest lapse into old ways. Similarly, Sylvester McCoy was accompanied by the spiky, confrontational Ace, who made an impression in her first full adventure as a travelling companion ('Remembrance of the Daleks', 1988) by battering a Dalek with a baseball bat. She also kept a stock of home-made nitroglycerine which she took great delight in using whenever given the chance. Sophie Aldred, who played Ace, has commented that 'the companions have always been a product of their age'[6] and it is hard to imagine the writers of 1980s *Doctor Who* (or for that matter, the modern show) getting away with introducing a character as timid and unempowered as Victoria (1967–1968). Significantly, the first scream in the 2005 series is from the male half of a couple in the pizza restaurant in 'Rose'. Rose herself does not scream until the fifth episode, 'World War Three', despite a few earlier gasps and two separate instances of shouting for help while banging on a locked door.

Moral Compass

The Doctor's original companions were his grand-daughter Susan, and two of her Earth schoolteachers, Ian and Barbara. The humans in the TARDIS often had the additional role of being moral policemen for the Doctor, rebuking him when his alien sensibilities led him to do something they considered wrong – the earliest example coming in 'An Unearthly Child' (1963), when Ian has to stop the Doctor from killing a wounded caveman who is slowing their party down, such was the urgency of his desire to get back to the TARDIS.

While later companions rarely had to keep the Doctor in check in this way, that probably reflects the evolution of the Doctor's character – later companions didn't do it, because later Doctors didn't need reminding that people's lives mattered. There is a sense in which Rose represents a revival of this tradition, scolding the Doctor for his disinterest in Mickey's apparent death in 'Rose' and rebuking him for his eagerness to kill van Statten's Dalek.

The New Crew

While Rose establishes herself as by far the most significant member of the TARDIS crew circa 2005, she is not the Doctor's only companion.

Jumping Jack Flash

Captain Jack Harkness is a former Time Agent from the fifty-first century, who first meets the Doctor while trying to pull off a confidence trick involving a Chula battlefield ambulance that he has scavenged in his own travels through time. At first Jack appears to be a glib, shallow and selfish buccaneer whom the Doctor taunts with undisguised contempt. Rose, her head turned by Jack's matinee-idol looks and silver-tongued charm, is more trusting – and perhaps that adds a sprinkling of jealousy into the Doctor's initial reaction to Jack.

But Jack proves his mettle at the end of 'The Doctor Dances', using his stolen space ship to prevent the German bomb from killing the Doctor, Rose and any number of former gas mask people. In turn, the Doctor comes to Jack's rescue, inviting him to join the TARDIS crew rather than stay on his ship and be blown out of the sky when the bomb finally explodes. Obviously the Doctor was unwilling to simply leave Jack to his fate, whatever character defects the younger man appeared to possess, but there is also a sense that the Doctor has seen the potential for Jack to prove himself a better man than he first appeared. The defining note on Jack's character comes as he walks into the TARDIS and comments, 'Much bigger on the inside', to which the Doctor replies, 'You'd better be.' When Jack later says, 'I wish I'd never met you, Doctor, I was much better off as a coward' ('Parting of the Ways'), it is clear that he doesn't mean what he says, and that he has lived up to the Doctor's hopes.

Jack is a latter-day example of the companion who frees the writers up to include the type of violence which the Doctor is either physically or temperamentally unable to carry out. The Doctor throws away his gun in 'Bad Wolf', berating the staff of the Games Station: 'as if I was ever going to fire', but we have no doubt that Jack would not be so squeamish. Similarly, while the Doctor seeks a characteristically technological solution to the impending Dalek invasion of Earth in 'Parting of the Ways', Jack seems equally at home organising the foot-soldiers in their defence to buy time for the Doctor.

Although Jack is left behind when the Doctor departs with Rose to regenerate into David Tennant, the door has been left open for his return at some point in the future (or, indeed, the past!).

The Companion Who Couldn't

'Imagine if you could get out there, travel among the stars and see it for real.' Brimming with youthful enthusiasm, Adam Mitchell was always likely to volunteer for a tour of duty in the TARDIS. Add this to his self-confessed genius and he looks like the ideal recruit, but this is far from the truth of the matter.

Russell T. Davies' original pitch document, prepared to outline his plans for the 2005 series for the benefit of BBC executives and scriptwriters alike, gives episode seven the working title of 'The Companion Who Couldn't'.[7] Adam, for all his intelligence, has much more trouble than Rose in getting his head around the implications of time travel. More significantly, he quickly loses whatever trust the Doctor had in him when he attempts to send the secrets of futuristic technology back home to his mother's telephone answering machine. In the classic years of *Doctor Who*, it often seemed as if anybody who happened to wander into the TARDIS could become a companion. The 2005 version is much clearer on the very high standards that the Doctor insists on: 'I only take the best. I've got Rose.'

Left Behind

Another new development of the 2005 show is showing the impact that travelling with the Doctor has on the people left behind. Rose's boyfriend Mickey and her mother Jackie are important in reminding the audience that Rose hasn't always been a traveller in the fourth dimension, and that she has a past and people who miss her while she's away. In previous series, this fact has been glossed over in a number of ways – several characters join up with the Doctor because they are orphaned (Victoria; Nyssa) or feel that they have nothing left to keep them at home (Adric, 1980–1982). Others blunder into the TARDIS by mistake (Ian and Barbara, 1963–1965; Tegan) and while they express a desire to get back home, we never discover anything about that home. One way or another, a line tends to be drawn under a companion's life story, and the audience is encouraged to think of them only in terms of their current life in the TARDIS. Russell T. Davies has commented that he doesn't think audiences in 2005 would accept that way of thinking:

> In the old days it was travel or nothing with the Doctor. You'd sort of get on board the TARDIS and that's it, you were gone. And now I don't believe you'd watch the series without asking the basic common sense questions like: Don't her family miss her? Has she gone missing? Who loves her? Who's left behind?[8]

Mickey's situation is particularly difficult. Although when we first meet him, his narrow-minded rejection of the Doctor as 'an alien, a thing' serves as a contrast with Rose, whose openness demonstrates her suitability as a companion, by the end of 'World War Three' Mickey has shown his worth, won the Doctor round and been invited to join the TARDIS crew. But Mickey knows himself well enough to realise that a life of adventuring isn't for him. He also knows that a part of him will always be following Rose around. He can't go with her, and he can't just forget her. Rose's encounter with the Doctor has ruined Mickey's life.

Mickey provides a great deal of comic relief, almost causing the Doctor to lose Margaret Slitheen and earning the regular epithet of 'Mickey the Idiot', but his role in the show is far more significant than that. Along with Rose, he grounds the ongoing story, providing a context for us to understand Rose and to understand how strong her desire to travel with the Doctor is. If she didn't have anything pulling her to stay, we would never realise just how much being with the Doctor means to her.

The Old Girl

The final member of the Doctor's team is easily over-looked – the TARDIS. As long ago as the very first episode of the show in 1963, it has been established that the TARDIS is a living thing rather than just a machine. In 'The End of the World' the Doctor tells Rose that the TARDIS is telepathic, and when Margaret Slitheen is regressed to an egg, the Doctor's comments make it clear that when she looked into the beams of light from the heart of the TARDIS, she was meeting with another sentient being, rather than merely being exposed to a mechanical process. When Rose attempts something similar, she describes the experience by saying that 'I looked into the TARDIS, and the TARDIS looked into me'.

Over the years, the Doctor has occasionally had the opportunity to trade up, to replace his idiosyncratic, troublesome TARDIS with a newer model – one with a functional chameleon circuit, or which consistently took you to precisely the place and time you were aiming for. He has always allowed such opportunities to pass him by. In 'Boom Town', the Doctor describes the TARDIS as being more than 'just any old power source. It's the TARDIS – *my* TARDIS, the best ship in the Universe'. There is more than a hint that somehow the secrets of the universe are to be found hidden inside the panels of that battered old Police Box. The godlike powers that Rose discovers after looking into the time vortex could possibly be taken to support such a view.

The Doctor's oldest travelling companion is also instrumental in enabling Rose to save the day by defeating the Dalek fleet. The godlike being who claims to 'create myself', and to 'see the whole of time and space' may inhabit Rose's body, but the unearthly voice that utters those words leaves open the possibility that the Bad Wolf is the TARDIS as much as it is Rose.

The New Girl

For all the extra dimensions that Jack, Mickey, Adam and the TARDIS bring to the 2005 show, it is still Rose who is the most significant of the new companions, and there are many ways in which she expands the previous model of side-kick and transforms it into something new.

First of all, Rose seems to come to the Doctor's rescue (rather than vice versa) far more than companions of the past did. In 'Rose', the Doctor is helpless in the grip of the Autons until Rose remembers her junior school gymnastics and swings into action to rescue him. In 'Dalek', when the Doctor's traumatised anger threatens to overcome his reason, it is Rose who brings him back in line. Most dramatically of all, in 'Parting of the Ways' Rose's arrival, cosmic powers and all, not only deals decisively with the Dalek menace, it does so at a point when the Doctor has given up hope for himself and the entire human race.

Eccleston has commented, rightly, that 'Rose is the Doctor's equal in every way – apart, possibly, from his scientific knowledge.'[9] Unlike previous companions, there is a genuine sense of partnership between the two. There are elements of the partnership where the Doctor remains the senior – his lectures to her about her meddling with history in 'Father's Day' for example – but nevertheless, the dynamic between the two of them has a very different feel to anything that we have seen before. There may have been hints in the past of something more than mere affection, such as the bitter-sweet reaction of Jon Pertwee's Doctor to the news that Jo was leaving UNIT to marry Professor Jones ('The Green Death', 1973), but his attitude towards Jo always had more than a hint of the paternal to it. This is different. The Doctor has stared death in the face with countless companions before now, but he never told any of them 'I'm so glad I met you' as he does in the basement morgue in 'The Unquiet Dead'. He never gives any of them a farewell like the holographically expressed sentiments of 'Parting of the Ways'. The Doctor and Rose present us with a love story told across the length and breadth of time, a story that begins with held hands in the basement of Hendrik's, that develops to an embrace as Rose swings to the Doctor's rescue in the Nestene Consciousness' lair, to dancing in war-torn London and finally to a life-saving kiss in 'Parting of the Ways'.

The introduction of the back-story about the Doctor's experiences in the Time War make Eccleston a more damaged Doctor than at any time in his past. He may be defensive and full of the survival guilt that we discussed in Chapter 2, but he is also lonely. Rose's boredom and the Doctor's loneliness provide the perfect setting for both of them to discover a deeper relationship than anything that either of them had ever known. Throughout the series, Rose repeatedly denies that the Doctor is her boyfriend, asserting in 'Aliens of London' that, 'He's not my boyfriend, Mickey, he's better than that, he's much more important.'

How this intense relationship survives the Doctor's latest regeneration remains, at the time of writing, to be seen. What is clear is that in Rose the 2005 show has finally produced a companion for the Doctor who is more partner than side-kick, and who has had as pronounced an effect on his life as he has on hers.

Notes

[1] Noel Clarke, *Doctor Who Confidential: I Get A Side-kick Out Of You* (BBC3, first broadcast 16 April 2005).

[2] Russell T. Davies on *Doctor Who Confidential: I Get A Side-kick Out Of You*.

[3] Peter Davison on *Doctor Who Confidential: I Get a Side-kick Out Of You*.

[4] Janet Fielding quoted in Benjamin Cook, 'Mouth Almighty', *Doctor Who Magazine* (2 March 2005), p. 13.

5   Janet Fielding, 'Mouth Almighty', p. 18.
6   Sophie Aldred on *Doctor Who Confidential: I Get A Side-kick Out Of You*.
7   'Pitch Perfect', in *Doctor Who Magazine: Special Edition – Doctor Who Companion Series One* (July 2005), p. 47.
8   Russell T. Davies on *Doctor Who Confidential: I Get A Side-kick Out Of You*.
9   Christopher Eccleston on *Doctor Who Confidential: I Get A Side-kick Out Of You*.

4. *Doctor Who* 2005: Episode Guide

'You seem to know what's going on.'
'I give that impression, yeah.'
Stuart and the Doctor in 'Father's Day'

Episode One: 'Rose'

*First broadcast Saturday 26 March 2005,
written by Russell T. Davies.*

Rose Tyler leads a normal life working in a London department store, hanging out with her boyfriend Mickey and seemingly going nowhere. Then one day she is attacked by animated shop-window dummies (Autons) in the store basement but is rescued by a mysterious stranger who introduces himself as 'the Doctor' before blowing up the shop.

Intrigued, Rose searches for more information about the Doctor on the Internet, and meets up with conspiracy theorist Clive, who has tracked the Doctor's appearances throughout history. Sadly, when the Autons finally go on a killing spree, Clive is out shopping with his family, and he becomes their first victim.

The Autons are controlled (via a relay hidden in the London Eye) by the Nestene Consciousness, an alien with the ability to manipulate plastic (which previously appeared in 1970's 'Spearhead From Space' and 1971's

'Terror of the Autons'). With Rose's help (and not before Mickey has been swallowed by a wheelie bin and replaced with an Auton) the Doctor tracks the Nestene Consciousness to its lair and gives it one last chance to leave humanity alone. When Autons grab the Doctor, he is only saved by Rose's willingness to risk all on a wild rope swing.

Rose obviously impresses the Doctor and he invites her – but not Mickey – to join him in his travels. At first she declines, but the TARDIS rematerialises seconds later, and Rose accepts the Doctor's offer at the second time of asking.

This episode introduces the idea of the Time War, and begins the slow revelation of the Doctor's role in it. Although there is also a Time War in the books that sprang up to fill the gap once the BBC cancelled the old *Doctor Who*, Russell T. Davies says that his Time War has nothing to do with it.

Episode Two: 'The End of the World'

*First broadcast Saturday 2 April 2005,
written by Russell T. Davies.*

The Doctor and Rose arrive to witness the destruction of the world, some five billion years in the future. The Doctor uses his 'slightly psychic' paper to bluff himself and Rose into an exclusive party watching the event on Platform One. He also supercharges Rose's phone so that it can be used across the length of time and space (but you should see the bill at the end of the month).

There, our heroes meet a number of dignitaries including Jabe, a tree from the Forest of Cheem who is surprised to discover that the Doctor is a Time Lord, having believed them all to have perished in the Time War. The guest of honour is Cassandra, the last human (albeit one who is little more than a brain in a jar and a stretched piece of skin, prompting Rose to describe her as 'a bitchy trampoline'). Despite having had 708 separate surgical procedures, Cassandra considers herself a pure human, in contrast to others from Earth who 'mingled' with other species resulting in what Cassandra dismisses as 'mongrels'.

Someone sabotages the computers so that the radiation from the expanding sun will destroy Platform One. Jabe gives her life in helping the Doctor to get them back online. The scheming villain of the piece turns out to be Cassandra, motivated purely by financial gain. As the Doctor says, 'Five billion years and it still comes down to money.'

When Rose aggressively challenges the Doctor to tell her more about himself, he refuses to be drawn on his background, and we see the first signs of the emotional scars that he carries.

The first example of the 'Bad Wolf' teaser running through the series is found when the Moxx of Balhoon describes the sabotage as being 'the Bad Wolf scenario'.

Episode Three: 'The Unquiet Dead'

First broadcast Saturday 9 April 2005,
written by Mark Gatiss.

More séance fiction than science fiction. The Doctor and Rose find themselves in 1869 Cardiff where undertaker Mr Sneed is facing a problem of reanimated corpses.

Sneed and his maid Gwyneth follow the formerly-late Mrs Peace to a theatre where Charles Dickens is appearing, but the old lady's body sparks a riot before they can recapture her.

In the chaos Rose is drugged and taken back to Sneed's, hotly pursued by the Doctor and his new side-kick, Charles Dickens. Gwyneth's second sight turns out to be caused by a weak point, or rift, in time and space located underneath the building. The Doctor persuades Gwyneth to hold a séance, and discovers the presence of the Gelth: a disembodied alien race, victims of the Time War. Stripped of their bodies and existing only in a gaseous state, the Gelth are desperate to use human cadavers to ensure their survival. Despite Rose's protestations, the Doctor offers to help and Gwyneth agrees to form a bridge across the rift for the Gelth.

But the Gelth lied. There are millions of them, and they don't just want to go to a new home, they want 'this world and all its flesh'. With the Doctor and Rose cornered by a horde of zombies in the morgue, Dickens realises that flooding the room with gas will drive the Gelth out of the corpses. While everybody else gets clear, Gwyneth holds the aliens in the building and blows it apart by lighting a match in the gas-filled room.

Despite some complaints about the presence of a séance on early evening television, there is nothing in tone or subject in this episode which would have been out of place in classic *Doctor Who* episodes such as 'The Masque of Mandragora' (1976) or 'The Talons of Weng Chiang' (1977).

Gwyneth's second sight gives her extraordinary insight into Rose's life, enabling her to know about the death of Rose's dad, and prompting her to remark that Rose 'has flown so far – further than anyone. The things you've seen, the darkness, the big bad wolf'.

Episode Four: 'Aliens of London'

First broadcast Saturday 16 April 2005,
written by Russell T. Davies.

The first two-part story of the new series. The Doctor takes Rose home, but 12 months later than he thinks. Rose returns to Jackie's flat and discovers that her mother has been worried sick. In Rose's absence, Mickey was questioned five times by the suspicious police.

Rose and the Doctor witness an alien spaceship crash-land in the Thames, trashing Big Ben in the process. Unable to get near the crash scene, they watch developments on TV with Rose's family. When the Doctor discovers that a 'body of non-terrestrial origin' was recovered from the crash and taken to a nearby hospital, he slips away to investigate.

At the hospital, the Doctor discovers the 'alien' to be a technologically augmented pig, which is unceremoniously shot dead by a soldier at the hospital. The Doctor realises that the pig is a fake alien, but one which can only have been created with the use of genuine alien technology.

Meanwhile, with the Prime Minister mysteriously missing, a group of aliens pose as acting Prime Minister Joseph Green and his portly advisors. Another MP, Harriet Jones, witnesses the aliens killing senior Army officer General Asquith, and so discovers their ability to impersonate humans.

The Doctor and Rose go to 10 Downing Street and split up. Rose, Harriet Jones and Prime Ministerial aide Indra Ganesh discover the body of the Prime Minister in a Downing Street cupboard, and are found by Margaret Blaine, who reveals that she and her fellow aliens are 'the Slitheen'. At the same time, Jackie is attacked by a

Slitheen at her home and the Doctor realises that the meeting he has been summoned to attend is a trap to remove the experts who might know how to fight the aliens. Joseph Green Slitheen activates a deadly shock to kill all of the experts, and the credits roll with three separate groups under threat from the Slitheen – and the first cliff-hanger ending of the series.

Other points of note are the Doctor's assertion that he 'doesn't do families' and his claim to be 900 years old. While the TARDIS is parked outside Rose's block of flats, a young boy is seen writing graffiti on the side of the TARDIS – his chosen tag being 'Bad Wolf'.

The scene where the pig hammers on the door of its mortuary container is a parallel of our introduction to Paul McGann's Doctor in 1996's *Doctor Who: The Movie*.

Episode Five: 'World War Three'

First broadcast Saturday 23 April 2005,
written by Russell T. Davies.

The Doctor casts off his deadly name-tag and places it onto one of the Slitheen. This convulses all of the aliens, allowing the Doctor, Jackie (with Mickey's help), Rose and Harriet to escape. Indra Ganesh is killed by Margaret Slitheen.

The Doctor, Harriet and Rose are chased by soldiers and Slitheen respectively, before taking refuge together in the Cabinet Room, where they are protected by three-inch-thick armour plating in the walls.

The Doctor discovers that Slitheen is a surname, not a species. Their plan is to gain access to the security codes for Britain's nuclear missiles, start a World War that will reduce the Earth to radioactive waste and then sell off the remains to the highest bidder. The Doctor is appalled that the motivation for their actions is purely financial.

With help from Rose and Harriet, the Doctor identifies the Slitheen homeworld as Raxacoricofallapatorius, which tells him that they are vulnerable to acetic acid – vinegar. Armed with this information, Mickey and Jackie kill one with a cocktail of pickled onions, pickled eggs and gherkin juice from Mickey's kitchen. Acting under the Doctor's guidance, Mickey hacks into a Royal Navy website and orders a conventional missile attack on 10 Downing Street. Rose, the Doctor and Harriet survive the blast due to Rose's suggestion of taking cover in a sturdy cupboard. As Harriet takes charge of the aftermath, the Doctor remembers where he knows her name from – she is to become one of Britain's greatest Prime Ministers.

Jackie agrees to give the Doctor a chance, telling Rose to bring him round for a meal. But the Doctor is having none of it, and he leaves again in the TARDIS with Rose. Before leaving he offers Mickey the chance to come with them, but Mickey declines, recognising that the Doctor's way of life isn't for him.

Episode Six: 'Dalek'

First broadcast Saturday 30 April 2005,
written by Rob Shearman.

2012: The Doctor and Rose respond to a distress signal and arrive at a museum of alien artefacts, deep underground in Utah. The museum is the property of multi-millionaire Henry van Statten, who scavenges alien technology to make a fortune from patents. One of his staff is Adam, a young Englishman whose job is to locate and buy alien devices at auctions across the world.

Van Statten asks the Doctor to shed light on his only living exhibit, a strange metal-encased creature dubbed 'Metaltron'. The Doctor swiftly discovers it to be a Dalek who somehow survived the Time War. The Dalek is weakened and powerless, until it feeds off Rose's DNA (more potent than normal human DNA because of her travels in time) and is able to reconstruct its cells and regenerate itself.

The Dalek breaks free and runs amok in the underground complex, killing vast numbers of guards. In a desperate attempt to contain the Dalek, the Doctor activates the security bulkheads. Adam gets out in time, but Rose is trapped. When the Doctor discovers that the Dalek has spared Rose's life, he agrees to open the bulkhead for them both.

The Doctor seems genuinely shaken by this unexpected encounter with his oldest enemy, and is so set on killing it that at one point the Dalek tells him 'you would make a good Dalek'.

But the Dalek is changing as a result of absorbing Rose's DNA, and the human side of the new hybrid Dalek/human begins questioning itself. Rose prevents the Doctor from killing the Dalek, and he explains that the Dalek is mutating into something new. This concept horrifies the Dalek, who sees its new form as sickness rather than life. It asks Rose to order it to die. She reluctantly agrees and the Dalek exterminates itself.

At the end of the episode, van Statten's employees turn on him, treating him to the same memory-wiping that he has inflicted on so many of their colleagues over the years. The Doctor invites Adam to join the crew of the TARDIS.

Henry van Statten's helicopter has the call sign 'Bad Wolf One'.

Episode Seven: 'The Long Game'

First broadcast Saturday 7 May 2005,
written by Russell T. Davies.

The Doctor, Rose and Adam arrive on Satellite Five, a space station in the year 200,000 during the fourth great and bountiful human empire.

While Rose and Adam explore, the Doctor discovers that Satellite Five is a news broadcast station. The TARDIS travellers watch a demonstration, discovering that the journalists use computer implants to process the news directly through their own brains. Adam is impressed, but the Doctor knows that something is wrong.

The Doctor isn't the only one to notice something that doesn't fit. The Editor realises that one of the journalists, Suki, has a false biography – she is a freedom fighting anarchist working undercover. He has her 'promoted' to floor 500, confronts her, has her killed and then put back to work.

Adam uses the unlimited credit that the Doctor gave him to have an Info Spike installed in his own head. He wants to phone home with details of futuristic technology.

On floor 500, the Editor captures the Doctor and Rose, telling them that humanity is enslaved by the Mighty Jagrafess of the Holy Hadrojassic Maxarodenfoe, who maintains power by the complete manipulation of the news media. Humanity has lost the ability to ask questions, simply accepting whatever they are told.

The Doctor refuses to answer questions, but the Editor discovers everything when Adam activates his new Info Spike.

Cathica, a journalist goaded into breaking out of her conditioning by the Doctor, enables Rose and the Doctor to escape. When Cathica vents all the heat in the satellite to floor 500, the Jagrafess overheats and explodes. Rose and the Doctor run, while Suki grabs the Editor and stops him from escaping.

The Doctor takes Adam back home, destroys the telephone answering machine with his downloaded secrets, and leaves him. He warns Adam to live a quiet, average life, because if anyone ever discovers his chip, they will dissect him.

One of the TV channels glimpsed on Satellite Five is called 'Bad Wolf TV'.

Episode Eight: 'Father's Day'

First broadcast Saturday 14 May 2005,
written by Paul Cornell.

Rose and the Doctor go back in time to meet Rose's father, Pete Tyler, who died in 1987. First they attend Pete and Jackie's wedding, then Rose persuades the Doctor to take her to the day Pete dies. Rose hesitates and misses her chance to be at Pete's side at the fatal moment, and she asks the Doctor to let her try again.

This time Rose doesn't falter – but rather than just talk, she pushes Pete out of the way of the speeding car and saves his life. Rose's actions (coupled with the double presence of the time travellers) creates a wound in time, allowing Reapers loose on Earth. The Doctor describes Reapers as being like bacteria, cleaning the wound by consuming everything in it. The Doctor thinks Rose planned to save her father all along, and angrily threatens to leave. But when he returns to the TARDIS he discovers that the inside has vanished – it is just a normal sized empty Police Box.

Rose accompanies Pete to a wedding, noticing several mistakes in the time-line along the way, including the repeated appearance and disappearance of the car that was supposed to kill Pete. At the wedding, several guests are inexplicably missing, and Rose sparks off a row between her parents (Jackie thinks Rose is Pete's latest fling). The young Mickey is in a playground, but he runs for safety when the other children are snatched by Reapers.

Reapers appear, and the Doctor orders everyone to take cover in the church. Rose's Dad starts to work out what is going on, and as the Doctor attempts to restore the TARDIS, Pete questions Rose about the future. He realises that his averted death is the cause of the Reapers' appearance. When Jackie overhears Pete say he is Rose's Dad, she starts another argument, which results in the adult Rose touching her infant self. This creates another paradox, and enables the Reapers to appear inside the church.

The Doctor is devoured by a Reaper, which then flies into the regenerating TARDIS. Both disappear. With the Doctor dead and the TARDIS gone, Rose realises that there is no hope for the entire world.

Pete sees the temporally displaced car again, and runs in front of it. When the car hits him, the Reapers vanish and the Doctor reappears at Rose's side, telling her to go to her father quickly. She reaches Pete just before he dies. Everyone else who was killed has reappeared, and time is back on its proper course.

When Rose and the Doctor are first seen in 1987, the words 'Bad Wolf' are scrawled across a fly poster for a rave.

Episode Nine: 'The Empty Child'

First broadcast Saturday 21 May 2005,
written by Steven Moffatt.

The first episode of a two-parter. The Doctor is pursuing an unidentified alien craft through time and space, his attention drawn by its mauve alert distress signal. The TARDIS materialises in London in the height of the blitz.

While the Doctor gets nowhere asking the audience in a nightclub whether anyone has seen anything falling from the sky recently, an air raid begins and Rose tries to rescue a young boy in a gas mask from a nearby rooftop. She climbs a rope, finds herself clinging to an untethered barrage balloon and begins to regret her choice of a Union Jack T-shirt. Ex-Time Agent Captain Jack Harkness rescues Rose, and woos her from his invisible space ship moored by Big Ben. Jack uses nanogenes to heal the rope burns on Rose's hands and attempts to sell her the alien craft that the Doctor is looking for.

The TARDIS phone rings – a surprise, as the Doctor says it doesn't work – and a young woman, Nancy, warns the Doctor not to answer it. He ignores her and hears a childish voice asking for its mummy.

The Doctor follows Nancy, who is using the cover of air raids to steal food for local homeless children. A knock at the window interrupts their meal, as the gas mask boy arrives, still calling for his mummy. The children run, and Nancy tells the Doctor not to let the boy touch him. Nancy says that her brother was killed in an air raid and sends the Doctor to talk to somebody who is also, apparently, called 'the Doctor'.

At Albion Hospital our Doctor meets Doctor Constantine. The hospital is full of victims of a strange plague: identical symptoms, including the fusing of a gasmask to the face, transmitted by touch alone. Constantine tells the Doctor that Nancy knows more than she is saying, before himself becoming a gas mask person.

Rose and Jack find the Doctor at the hospital, and the three of them are confronted with a ward of gasmask people closing in on them. Nancy returns to the food-laden deserted house, and is herself cornered by the boy, who she calls 'Jamie'. As the gas mask people advance, the credits roll.

During a conversation between Nancy and the Doctor, Nancy's comments about the Doctor having a big nose and big ears have parallels with the Big Bad Wolf in the fairy tale Little Red Riding Hood ('what big ears you have Grandma . . .').

Episode Ten: 'The Doctor Dances'

First broadcast Saturday 28 May 2005,
written by Steven Moffatt.

The Doctor tells the gas mask people off, ordering them to their room. All of them, including the one closing in on Nancy, obey the Doctor's command.

The Doctor accuses Jack of starting the plague. Jack argues that all he was doing was conning the Time Agents by selling them a soon-to-be-destroyed Chula battlefield ambulance. Exploring the room where the first victim was taken, they find signs of a struggle, dozens of childlike drawings on the walls, and recordings of Doctor Constantine's interviews with the child.

Nancy is caught by the owners of the house she has been raiding, and blackmails her way to freedom.

Nancy finds her gang of urchins and tells them that they shouldn't depend on her, explaining that the gasmask boy is looking for her.

Back at the hospital, the Doctor, Rose and Jack run from the gas mask boy, using Jack's sonic blaster to remove walls, but they are soon trapped in a dead-end. Jack teleports himself out of danger, and reconfigures his ship's emergency teleport to rescue Rose and the Doctor. His stolen ship, like the ambulance, is Chula in design. He tells Rose and the Doctor that he left the Time Agents when he realised that two years of his memories had been erased.

Nancy is caught by the soldiers at the bombsite. Despite her protests, they leave her tied up with a soldier, who she realises is succumbing to the plague. She pleads with him to release her, but before her eyes he turns into a gas mask person.

The Doctor, Rose and Jack go to the bombsite. Jack knows the guard, Algy, to be gay, so Jack (rather than Rose) goes to distract him. The Doctor explains to Rose that by the fifty-first century, humans are more flexible about who they 'dance' with. Algy becomes the latest plague victim, and the Doctor frees Nancy, who kept her guard at bay by singing lullabies.

Then the group sets off a distress signal from the ambulance which summons all of the gas mask people. The Doctor explains that the nanogenes from the ambulance tried to heal the first thing they encountered – a dead human child wearing a gas mask. With no past knowledge of human biology, they did the best they could – using the gas-mask-wearing child as their blueprint for remaking the rest of humanity. Jack realises that the Doctor has been right all along – he caused the plague.

When Jamie arrives, Nancy admits that she isn't his sister, she is his mummy. They embrace, and the nanogenes recognise the family DNA and correctly reconfigure Jamie. The Doctor sets them to work restoring all the other victims of the plague.

Jack uses his spaceship to stop the German bomb, but is unable to either jettison it or teleport himself to safety. He resigns himself to death, until the Doctor lands the TARDIS on his ship and invites him aboard, where the newly expanded TARDIS crew dance the years away.

When Jack is seen suspended in mid-air, straddling the German bomb, the bomb has 'Schlechter Wolf' written on it – an approximation of Bad Wolf in German.

Episode Eleven: 'Boom Town'

First broadcast Saturday 4 June 2005,
written by Russell T. Davies.

The team meet up with Mickey in modern day Cardiff. The plan is to recharge the TARDIS using the time rift from 'The Unquiet Dead'. They are enjoying a café meal when the Doctor sees a local newspaper – Margaret Blaine (née Slitheen) has been elected Lord Mayor, which means trouble.

The four go to see Margaret (who escaped the Downing Street explosion by emergency teleport), and discover her plan to build a nuclear power station in Cardiff. It is designed to explode and provide the energy that Margaret needs to leave Earth, riding the shockwave on her Tribophysical Waveform Extrapolator ('a pan-dimensional surfboard'). She has already killed several people who got too close to discovering her latest scheme.

Margaret is quickly caught and the Doctor realises that the name of the proposed power station, Blaidd Drwg, is Welsh for Bad Wolf. This is the first time that the Doctor or Rose directly comment on the many Bad Wolf references that are following them. The Doctor takes Margaret to the TARDIS, intending to take her to face trial on Raxacoricofallapatorius. Margaret says that her entire family has been sentenced to execution with no appeal – if the Doctor takes her home, he condemns her to certain death.

Mickey and Rose slip away to talk about their relationship, and discover that things have changed too much to make it work. The Doctor agrees to take Margaret for a final meal, where she makes several attempts at killing him, all of which he effortlessly foils. Suddenly, the time rift reopens, with the TARDIS at the centre of the power storm – Margaret's back-up plan involved rigging the Extrapolator as a booby trap. Time and space are being ripped apart.

Rose, the Doctor and Margaret all run back to the TARDIS, and Margaret grabs Rose as a hostage, forcing the Doctor and Jack to set her free. Suddenly, a panel opens and Margaret stares into a strange light – the heart of the TARDIS, which the Doctor also describes as its soul. She regresses to an egg, and the Doctor takes her to the hatcheries on Raxacoricofallapatorius, giving her the fresh start she had pleaded for.

Once the disaster has been averted, Rose hurries to find Mickey amid the battered chaos of Cardiff. He sees her, but chooses to slip away without being found. Rose returns to the TARDIS and leaves with the Doctor and Jack, saying that Mickey deserves better.

Episode Twelve: 'Bad Wolf'

First broadcast Saturday 11 June 2005,
written by Russell T. Davies.

The first instalment in a two-part story. The Doctor suddenly finds himself an unwilling participant in the reality TV show *Big Brother*. Rose takes part in *The Weakest Link*, while Jack appears on *What Not To Wear*. All three discover that the shows have a deadly twist, with unsuccessful contestants being killed on air. The TV shows are broadcast from the Games Station, owned by the Bad Wolf Corporation, and broadcasting from the old Satellite Five (which the Doctor visited 100 years ago in episode seven).

Jack and the Doctor escape from their respective shows, the Doctor taking another contestant, Lynda, with him. Rose reaches the final, before losing to Rodrick. Jack and the Doctor rush in to rescue Rose, but are too late. They witness Rose being gunned down by the host of the show, Anne Droid.

The Doctor, Jack and Lynda are arrested, but escape and make their way to the broadcast control centre. One of the programmers reveals a history of unauthorised transmissions. Jack finds the TARDIS and uses it to discover that losing contestants are not disintegrated, but are transported somewhere else – Rose is still alive.

The Controller (who uses Info Spike technology to oversee broadcast operations) takes advantage of an interruption in transmissions to tell the Doctor that humanity is under the control of 'her masters', who have been in hiding for years. They fear the Doctor, which is why she found him and hid him in the games, where he wouldn't be noticed.

The Controller gives the Doctor the coordinates of her masters' hiding place, and is teleported away to be killed – by the Daleks. The Doctor discovers a Dalek fleet hidden in space: 200 ships, with more than 2,000 Daleks on each ship – an invasion force of almost half a million Daleks.

The Daleks warn the Doctor that unless he leaves them alone, they will exterminate Rose. He tells them that he's going to rescue Rose, save the Earth and wipe the Daleks from the sky. The Daleks escalate their plans for the invasion of Earth, and the credits roll.

Episode Thirteen: 'The Parting of the Ways'

First broadcast Saturday 18 June 2005,
written by Russell T. Davies.

The Doctor and Jack pilot the TARDIS onto the Dalek flagship, avoiding a missile attack. They materialise around Rose and a Dalek, who Jack outguns. Protected by a force field, the Doctor talks to the Daleks. He discovers that the Emperor Dalek survived the Time War, and has spent years breeding new Daleks from human cells. He has also gone mad, styling himself as the god of the Daleks.

The Doctor and company return to the Games Station, while the Dalek fleet mobilises. Jack takes command of the satellite defences, while the Doctor and Rose start building a Delta Wave to destroy the Daleks. The Doctor tricks Rose into the TARDIS and sends her home – he knows the situation is hopeless, and doesn't want her to die. He has left a pre-recorded holographic message telling Rose not to try to come back, and to have a great life.

The Emperor Dalek taunts the Doctor, knowing that if the Delta Wave works, it will also destroy all life on Earth. The Doctor asks how the Daleks sent the words 'Bad Wolf' through time and space, but the Emperor denies all knowledge.

Back home, an inconsolable Rose meets Mickey and Jackie. When she notices prominent 'Bad Wolf' graffiti she realises that Bad Wolf isn't a warning, it's a message telling her to go back to the Doctor. With renewed purpose, she tries to open the heart of the TARDIS, hoping that it will read her intentions.

The Daleks attack the Games Station, and one by one Jack and his defenders are killed. The Doctor is surrounded by Daleks and taunted by the Emperor – can he bring himself to use the Delta Wave? Is he a killer or a coward? The Doctor backs down, defeated.

But Rose arrives in the nick of time, with godlike powers bestowed on her by the TARDIS' time vortex. She explains that she is the Bad Wolf, and scatters those words throughout time and space as a self-fulfilling message to herself. She also restores Jack to life and scatters the Daleks' atoms, destroying the entire fleet.

But the Doctor knows that Rose's human body will not be able to cope with the time vortex's power for long. He kisses her and draws the power into his body. They leave in the TARDIS, (Jack arrives just in time to see it dematerialise). As Rose recovers, the Doctor explains to her that he is dying, but that he will regenerate into a new form. They share an emotional farewell, and a fierce burst of energy erupts from out of him. When it subsides a different Doctor stands in front of Rose. He muses on the weirdness of having new teeth, and begins the second era of new *Who*.

Part Two

5. You Lot

**An ordinary man – that's the most important
thing in creation.**
The Doctor in 'Father's Day'

Hard though it may be to believe, some people don't like science fiction. They feel that it is too remote from their day-to-day lives and addresses none of their concerns. Added to which, the dystopian nature of much science fiction has an alienating effect on some people. Yet somehow *Doctor Who* manages to draw in many of those who would generally be turned off by technology and science fiction. And not just draw them in, but get them strongly engaged in it. The reason is that, despite the constant presence of aliens and technology, *Doctor Who* is above all a story about us – humanity.

Russell T. Davies is very alert to the importance of audience psychology and says that he believed it was essential to make a strong connection with the viewers:

> One of the problems of *Doctor Who* is, its greatest strength can be its greatest weakness, in that you've got the freedom to go anywhere in time and space, and that is wonderful and liberating. It can also get annoying because it means there's no anchor, there's no connection to the people watching, which is very, very important.[1]

Davies is more committed to telling the story well and making an emotional impact on the audience than being rigorously consistent with previous series. He's also more concerned about this than maintaining the internal logic of the stories. After all, the programmes exist primarily to entertain, and the BBC wants to reach a broad audience. That will only happen in so far as the viewers are constantly drawn in at an emotional level, and made to feel strongly for the characters within the series. Davies says, 'You've got to get emotion into this stuff . . . good, honest, heartfelt emotion.'[2] This would be difficult to achieve if the lead characters did not at least seem human. In the world of animated cartoons, for example, animators work extremely hard to give their main characters recognisably human characteristics so that viewers can identify with them. The Doctor's human form is not just so that the programme is easier to make – it makes him particularly easy to relate to. The fact that he is a Gallifreyan with two hearts, the ability to regenerate, and an extraordinary intelligence is, most of the time, neither here nor there to us. We feel like he is one of us. In fact, not only does he look just like us, he also has what seem to be some very human foibles. So we put to one side the fact that he is an alien, and instead perhaps tend to view him as an extreme version of a human. And yet, at the same time, it is also true that the Doctor's alien perspective on human beings enables us to see ourselves and our society in a fresh light.

A further aspect of the drive to emotionally involve the viewers is in the nature of the storylines. Davies was insistent that, for the first series at least, the stories should all centre on our world. Quite literally, it earths the series, giving viewers locations and characters that they can instantly connect with. This is why the Doctor and Rose keep returning to her home. Davies explains why:

> Storywise it feels good – it grounds it again. You can go to the end of the universe so long as you come back. If you just go to the end of the universe and stay there, you've lost it.[3]

At first glance, 'The End of the World' (episode 2), gives us familiarity of neither locations nor humans – the scenes did not take place on Earth, and the last human was unrecognisable as one of our species. But it was very obviously our story. It's the end of our line and of our home. At the end of the episode, the Doctor stands with Rose in a busy street and ties it back to our own context:

> You think it will last for ever: people and cars and concrete. But it won't. One day it's all gone – even the sky.

So if *Doctor Who* is really all about us, just what is it telling us about ourselves?

Stupid Apes

'You lot' is one of the Doctor's common ways of being a little dismissive of human beings, lumping us all under one faintly derisory heading. Tom Baker's Doctor may have described humans as his 'favourite species', but you do wonder just how much of us the Doctor can take. His expectations of the humans he meets are always low, at least initially. Almost the first words the Doctor says to Rose are scornful. When she speculates about the Autons being students he gives her every opportunity to show how stupid she is, asking why she thinks that. When Rose eventually offers a plausible reason ('To get that many people dressed up and being silly, they've got to be students') the Doctor concedes 'That makes sense. Well done ... They're not students.' However, his recognition of some reasonable logic doesn't yet translate into thinking that Rose is anything more than another small-brained human. Moments later he waves his bomb at her and says:

> I'm going to go upstairs and blow it up. And I might well die in the process, but don't worry about me, no. You go home. Go on. Go and have your lovely beans on toast.

Clayton Hickman, editor of *Doctor Who Magazine*, says:

> The Doctor getting frustrated with Rose is nothing new. He always gets frustrated with his companions ... although he loves the human race – or professes to love the human race – he's never very patient with it. There are times when the Doctor's slightly unfair to his companions, or to those he's met. But I guess it just shows he's an alien and he doesn't really have the patience some of us do.[4]

He is certainly not very patient with people who he feels are too small-minded to grapple with the new realities to which he exposes them. He criticises humans for being closed-minded: 'You're happy to believe in something invisible, but if it's staring you in the face – nope, can't see it. There's a scientific explanation for that: you're thick' ('World War Three').

Again in 'Rose', the Doctor says he is 'trying to save every stupid ape blundering about on top of this planet.' To the Doctor's hyper-scientific mind, we seem to be barely distinguishable in any meaningful way from our closest animal relatives. He would know that

we share much of the same DNA with other primates
– 98.5% of the human genetic code is also common
to chimpanzees.[5] The description 'stupid apes' is one
which Eccleston's Doctor uses of us time and again.
Putting us on the same level as other apes presents
us as being profoundly limited by our all too brief
evolutionary history. The Doctor stresses this in 'Rose'
when he pleads with the Nestene Consciousness:

> This planet is just starting. These stupid little people have
> only just learned to walk, but they're capable of so much
> more.

We'll return to the potential which *Doctor Who* sees in
human beings shortly, but for now it's the fact that we
haven't been long on our feet which shows the Doctor's
view of humanity: babyish, clueless, self-absorbed and
needing a lot of looking after. He has a point. In the
amazing history of life on this planet, we are very
much the new kids on the block. Imagine all of Earth's
4.6 billion years of history taking place within 24
hours: life begins at 4 am, but with little change until
the evening. At almost 9 pm the first jellyfish appear;
around an hour later the first plants on land start to
grow, followed shortly after by the first land animals.
The dinosaurs are around from 11ish to 11.49, and
humans finally show up at one minute and seventeen
seconds to midnight.

In a very short period of time, humans have outgrown
their nursery, developing language, progressing the
simple tools of rocks and sticks into ever more elaborate
and diverse implements, and creating fabulously diverse
cultures and societies. Rocks and sticks were still the
technology of choice for the cavemen in the first *Doctor
Who* story in 1963. These were human beings at the very

dawn of civilisation, and the time-travelling Doctor is not only very aware of how quickly the human race has developed since then, but also of how close to primates we are in some ways. The Doctor may call us stupid apes, but he would also agree with many scientists that we are spectacularly clever apes, primarily thanks to the development of language.

Depends What You Mean by 'People'

Although the Doctor does lump us in with the apes, his concern is less with the biology of *Homo sapiens* than with a broader concept – that of a person. For the Doctor, there is nothing intrinsically special about us. We feel special because on this planet we are uniquely endowed.[6] But the Doctor has encountered equivalent species on other planets. When he and Rose arrive on Platform One to watch the end of the world, they hear the announcement to guests and Rose asks, 'So, when it says "guests" does that mean people?' 'Depends what you mean by people,' replies the Doctor. 'I mean people,' says Rose, 'what do you mean?' The Doctor's answer is simple and to the point: 'Aliens.' For the Doctor they are all people. Yasmin Bannerman, who plays Jabe, agrees saying, 'I wouldn't call us monsters because we're not monstrous. We're just different.'[7]

The faculties which go to make up 'a person' on Earth are the same faculties which make up 'a person' on Gallifrey or anywhere else. We don't doubt that the Doctor is a person, though he is undeniably inhuman. What makes him a person is not his physical appearance but something less tangible. However, some take a different view. For Cassandra pure human DNA is all-important – this alone is what makes one a person.

Cassandra tells Rose:

> I am the last pure human. The others mingled. Oh, they call themselves new humans and proto-humans and digi-humans – even humanish. But do you know what I call them? Mongrels.

Rose, understandably, finds Cassandra such a distorted representation of humanity that she exclaims:

> You're not human. You've had it all nipped and tucked until there's nothing left. Anything human got chucked in the bin. You're just skin, Cassandra, lipstick and skin.

But while Rose has a point in suggesting that Cassandra has lost something essentially human, she doesn't suggest that she's no longer a person – just that she's not a very nice one. When the Doctor reverses Cassandra's teleportation device and brings her back, he says, 'People have died, Cassandra. You murdered them.' Cassandra doesn't challenge the facts themselves, but the Doctor's interpretation of them:

> It depends on your definition of 'people'. And that's enough of a technicality to keep your lawyers dizzy for centuries.

Peter Singer, Professor of Bioethics at Princeton University, insists on the distinction between a human and a person: a human is a member of the species *Homo sapiens*; a person is any being with self-consciousness and rationality. In his influential book *Rethinking Life and Death*, Singer starts one chapter with a shocking account of the outrageous mistreatment of people in an experimental lab – and then reveals that the 'people' involved are actually chimpanzees.[8] It's a clever and effective way to make his point that what really matters is *personhood* not *humanity*. He goes on to argue that a newborn baby has no self-consciousness and no rationality, and therefore is *not yet* a person, whereas an adult chimpanzee has a measure of self-consciousness and rationality, and therefore *is* a person. Which has the greater right to life? For Singer it's the person – the chimp. He argues that it should be as legitimate to 'terminate' a newborn baby which has some disability as it is to terminate an unborn fœtus:

> It's a terrible thing to kill someone who wants to live; it's a terrible thing to kill a newborn infant against its parents' wishes. But if they don't want the child to live, if the child's prospects are blighted and they think it's better that it not live, then, I think, it's not a terrible thing.[9]

It's a powerful – though fundamentally flawed – argument. We will return to why we think it's flawed shortly. The Doctor and Singer seem to share the same conviction that personhood, rather than a particular genome, is the critical thing – though it's hard to imagine the Doctor endorsing infanticide.

The Matter of the Heart

This focus on persons arises naturally out of the belief that the only reality is the physical universe. This belief, or worldview, goes under a couple of different names. Sometimes people refer to it as scientific materialism, expressing the idea that absolutely everything is purely matter and is therefore open to scientific investigation. It is also called philosophical naturalism (or just naturalism), expressing the idea that everything is natural; there is no supernatural (the philosophical bit helps to distinguish people who hold this worldview from the naturalists who study the natural world).

If it is true that there is nothing real except that which is physical, then human beings, too, are nothing but matter. It means that everything that goes on in our brains is physical; our minds are the way we experience what is happening there. Our self-consciousness, all our feelings, emotions and intuitions are simply particular mental states which are the results of activity within the brain. Even any sense of spiritual reality we might have is, in this view, simply a physical brain phenomenon. In fact, many researchers into consciousness – who start from a naturalist position – assume that what Christians and other religious people mean by the human 'spirit' is just another way of talking about the mind. In other words, every aspect of our minds is caused by the particular structure of our brain and by external influences on us which produce certain signals within the brain. Our brain structure is determined by our genes and the combined effect of all the external influences on us since our brains first formed in the womb. So everything we think and feel is the product of our inherited DNA and the environmental influences on us – including our diet, how we were cared for and stimulated as children, our habits, the television programmes we have exposed our brains to, etc. And that makes everything deterministic – everything we think is the result of long chains of cause and effect within the physical world. And there is no place for freedom. What all this means is that we are nothing but complex biochemical systems which have an impressive ability to gather and process data about the surrounding world. We are nothing but animals with language.

The Heart of Matter

But is this enough to explain what we are really like? And is the idea of a 'person' being a creature with self-consciousness and rationality a good enough definition? Singer's reliance on these two defining characteristics (arguably two facets of the same thing) is far too limited. To start with, personhood is, in some ways, a transient thing, abandoning us every night when we sleep, or when we become unconscious for some reason. Singer says that we must allow for the latent personality within, which will return in due course. But maybe this simple fact suggests that it is an inadequate definition of a person. Secondly, it doesn't make enough allowance for the importance of the relational aspect of a person.[10]

Christians, in common with many religious traditions, also point to our spiritual dimension as a crucial component of what makes us persons. It's a dimension which Singer rules out from the start – as, on the whole, does *Doctor Who* (see Chapter 9). But it is a dimension which changes everything. If human beings do have a spiritual aspect, then personhood is defined by more than self-consciousness and rationality. And then, even if there is no rationality or self-consciousness (as in the case of a newborn infant), the individual nevertheless remains a person with intrinsic value. In 'The Ark In Space' (1975) companion Sarah-Jane is put into cryogenic suspended animation. Chief med-tech Vira asks, 'Is she of value?' to which Harry, the Doctor's other companion replies incredulously, 'Value? She's a human being like ourselves! What sort of question is that?' But if you go along with the view outlined above, the very concept of 'value' is meaningless. Values and morality are empty concepts if every thought which passes through our minds is nothing but the result of our DNA and external influences on us.

The Christian perspective is that human beings are of special value – not just because of our exceptional abilities compared to other species, but because we alone on Earth are made in God's image (the question of life elsewhere in the universe is covered in Chapter 11). The first chapter of the Bible, Genesis 1, is clear that God is the creator of everything, and that human beings are profoundly special. The questions of how long it took, and of the process by which we came to be, are largely irrelevant (though they are the cause of debate within Christian circles[11]). What matters is the theology which Genesis teaches: that we are not the result of a vast cosmic accident, and that we bear God's image. It is still true that there is continuity between us and other animals in that we do share a lot of DNA, our bodies work in the same way, and some of our human characteristics are just highly developed versions of animal characteristics. But being made in God's image means there is also a radical discontinuity. It's not about our humanoid shape, but about sharing something of God's attributes. Yes, we are self-conscious and rational, but we are also relational and creative, with genuine free will and moral responsibility. And we have this spiritual side, a capacity to experience the transcendent – something beyond physical reality. We are persons because God is personal. And of all physical life on Earth, that is only true of us humans.

Far from the Stars

As we have noted already, the Doctor is often dismissive of human lives and aspirations. Soon after he meets

Rose, he explains that he alone knows about, and is tackling, the plastic menace:

> Well, who else is there? I mean, you lot, all you do is eat chips, go to bed and watch the telly, while all the while underneath you there's a war going on.

Taken at face value, this is obviously untrue – we do lots of other things, like play cricket or visit nightclubs. But what the Doctor is suggesting is that human lives are trivial, restricted and banal in comparison with the enormous issues at stake beneath our very noses, but of which we are entirely ignorant. In the Doctor's mind, everything rests on him, the only saviour of the universe. There's something of a whiff of sour grapes about this. The way he says, 'Don't worry about me … Go home and have your lovely beans on toast' suggests that he feels like a martyr, getting no recognition or thanks, let alone any help.

When the Doctor takes Rose back to the day her father was killed, Rose intervenes and changes the course of history by saving his life. The Doctor is not at all pleased and suspects Rose of planning to do this from the time he first mentioned to her that the TARDIS is a time machine. He says to her:

> I did it again. I picked another stupid ape. I should have known. It's not about showing you the universe, it's about the universe doing something for you. ('Father's Day')

Here the Doctor's problem is not that Rose is failing to pull her weight in saving the universe, but that he interprets her actions as selfish ingratitude, using the Doctor and the TARDIS for her own ends rather than graciously submitting to her time-travelling tour guide. Paul Cornell, writer of 'Father's Day' says:

I think the Doctor is showing an alien quality here, in that he doesn't quite get how attached humans perhaps get to their families. On the other hand, as this episode reveals, he was fairly attached to his family himself.[12]

Henry van Statten is also criticised for being concerned with his own selfish agenda and so missing out of greater things. He claims that in hoarding all the alien technology (which he used to make vast profits) he 'wanted to touch the stars'. But the Doctor is having none of this: 'You just want to drag the stars down and stick them underground, underneath tons of sand and dirt, and label them. You're about as far from the stars as you can get.'

At other times, the Doctor is more indulgent of the ignorant vulnerability of the human species. In 'Rose' he comments that we 'have only just learned how to walk'. The fourth Doctor, commenting on how recently we 'crawled up out of the swamp', referred to us 'puny and defenceless bipeds', and the third Doctor justified his frequent visits to our planet by saying, 'Earth seems more vulnerable than others.' He may get impatient with our feeble minds, but he also recognises how limited our experience is.

To be fair to the Doctor, it's hardly surprising that he has a low view of us much of the time. In the 2005 series, he has to contend with Mickey's early preoccupation with self-preservation, the murderous arrogance of Cassandra, the ruthlessness and greed of Henry van Statten, the opportunism of Adam, the manipulative misuse of power on Satellite Five which enslaved the whole human race, the cowardice of most people there when the Daleks arrived, and much more besides. It's not a pretty picture, but it is one which is entirely consistent with the biblical view of human beings. We may be made in the image of God, but Genesis goes on to tell how human beings rebelled against God and introduced into our experience greed, deception, cowardice, slander, backbiting, rivalry, jealousy, violence, murder and more. In fact, the biblical position is that every human being is enslaved by this fundamental attitude of rebellion towards God. We may not be aware of it, of course, but that's not the point. When, in 'The Long Game' the Editor asked, 'Is a slave a slave if he doesn't know he's enslaved?', the Doctor had no hesitation in answering 'Yes'.

Capable of So Much More

There is another side to human beings too, which the Doctor clearly recognises. His response in 'Father's Day' when Stuart and Sarah say that they are not important reveals as much:

> Who says you're not important? I've travelled to all sorts of places, done things you couldn't even imagine. You two: street corner, two in the morning, getting a taxi home. I never had a life like that. Yes, I'll try to save you.

The Doctor clearly values the human capacity for relationship, our ability to express love. On a grander scale, in 'The Ark In Space' (1975) the Doctor sums up humanity's merits:

> *Homo sapiens*. What an inventive, invincible species ... They've survived flood, famine and plague. They've survived cosmic wars and holocausts, and now here they are out among the stars waiting to begin a new life, ready to outsit eternity. They're indomitable! Indomitable!

Doctor Who may show plenty of the dark side of human existence, but it also shows many of the positives.

Again this echoes the Christian understanding of human beings. Rebels we may be, but we are still bearers of the image of God. We have already commented on some aspects of this – rationality, creativity, morality, etc. All these and more are seen in *Doctor Who*. We have referred already to 'The Ark In Space', which provides an excellent example of how the classic series dealt with the issue of the human condition. When solar flares made the Earth inhospitable, thousands of humans went into space and were placed in suspended animation, awaiting the day when they could safely return to Earth and enable the human race to continue. However, an insect-like alien (called the Wirrn), discovers the space station, and identifies the preserved humans as hosts for growing its offspring. Noah, the leader of the humans, is transformed into a Wirrn, leads the alien swarm onto the transport ship and deliberately fails to set the stabilisers, resulting in the ship exploding. This averts the danger, and the only explanation is that his human self managed to reassert a degree of control over the Wirrn personality that had imprinted onto him. The Doctor comments that Noah's actions show 'more than a vestige of the human spirit'. As well as helping to explain what has happened to the audience, the Doctor's remark also serves as a recognition that human beings have high moral values at their very core.

The whole process of space exploration is an aspect of this too. The Doctor says that, 'Mankind goes into space to explore, to be part of something greater' ('Dalek'), but this is the wrong way round. Humanity explores because it is part of something greater. Part of the image of God is dominion over the natural world (not domination, though – there is no justification for environmental exploitation in the Bible). We are to look after it on God's behalf, and we are to occupy it and understand it. The fact that we have rational minds that are able to comprehend an understandable universe is not something to be taken lightly. As the great physicist Eugene Wigner said,

> The enormous usefulness of mathematics in the natural sciences is something bordering on the mysterious and there is no rational explanation for it. It is not at all natural that 'laws of nature' exist, much less that man is able to discover them. The miracle of the appropriateness of the language of mathematics for the formulation of the laws of physics is a wonderful gift which we neither understand nor deserve.

When the Doctor talks about a 'great and bountiful human empire' ('The Long Game'), it feels like something glorious. As it should be, because what he is talking about would be a marvellous expression of the urge to know, to understand, to create, to develop and to form communities in which people have all their needs met and in which they can fully express themselves. And that's a God-given thing.

Notes

[1] Russell T. Davies, *Doctor Who Confidential: Why On Earth?* (BBC3, first broadcast 23 April 2005).
[2] Russell T. Davies, *Doctor Who Confidential: Time Trouble* (BBC3, first broadcast 14 May 2005).
[3] Russell T. Davies, *Doctor Who Confidential: Why On Earth?*
[4] Clayton Hickman, *Doctor Who Confidential: Time Trouble*.
[5] We share more than 50% of our DNA with bananas but you don't hear people making much of that, even if the Doctor says that bananas are good.

6 cf. William A. Dembski, 'Reflections on Human Origins' at www.designinference.com/documents/2004.06.Human_ Origins.pdf.

7 Yasmin Bannerman, *Doctor Who Confidential: the Good, the Bad and the Ugly* (BBC3, first broadcast 2 April 2005).

8 Peter Singer, *Rethinking Life and Death* (Oxford University Press, 1994), p. 159.

9 Peter Singer, interviewed by Nelson González, 'Live and Let Die', *Third Way*, August 2002. Available online at www. damaris.org/content/content.php?type=5&id=96.

10 Singer acknowledges that the relational bond between a child and its parents is a significant factor in giving the baby its worth as a human being. So he suggests that there should be an upper limit of 28 days for infanticide as by this point the bond is becoming very strong. Perhaps he's never had children, since countless parents would say that the bond is instant, and many mothers would testify to a bond with their baby before birth.

11 cf. J.P. Moreland & John Mark Reynolds (eds.), *Three Views On Creation and Evolution* (Zondervan, 1999).

12 Paul Cornell, *Doctor Who Confidential: Time Trouble* (BBC3, first broadcast 14 May 2005).

6. Dancing with Death

**Everything has its time
and everything dies**
The Doctor in 'The End of the World'

'I think what makes it uniquely scary as a programme is that it's steeped in death,' says Russell T. Davies. 'The body count in the history of *Doctor Who* is extraordinary. It's a slaughter house.'[1] Death has been a constant factor since the first story ('An Unearthly Child', 1963) which took us back to the violent dawn of human culture. Since then the death toll has indeed been astronomical. 'Resurrection of the Daleks' (1984) has seven deaths within the first minute. Peter Davison says:

> The story of 'Resurrection of the Daleks' had, I think, a higher death count than *Terminator*. You know, gratuitously violent, people were being shot all over the place. It's quite extraordinary that we got away with it. They were mostly aliens so that doesn't matter, but still.[2]

The killing continues unabated in the 2005 series. While 'Boom Town' only shows one death (although it has the most discussion about death), 'Dalek' and 'Parting of the Ways' give the opportunity for vast killing sprees. Davies says, 'When I write [episodes] now I think, "Oh, it's twenty pages and no one's died, I'd better put a death in." So for all that life and energy [*Doctor Who* has] got, it's a very dark world. It's about death.'[3] We argued in the previous chapter that ultimately *Doctor Who* is about the nature of human beings, but of course death is an integral part of human existence. However, before we get into that issue, it is perhaps worth a brief look at the violence which so often leads to death within *Doctor Who*.

TV: A Killing Machine?

The concerns about the effects of television violence are naturally strongest when the audience for a programme includes children. These concerns are completely understandable even if people disagree on how influential television programmes are: the innocence of children is a precious thing which cannot be regained once it is lost. Added to which, many people feel that children are so easily influenced by what they see that they are easily corrupted. A programme maker always needs to carefully weigh up what kind of negative impact their programme could have on impressionable young minds. On the other hand, television channels must cater for a wide audience and it is unreasonable to expect a family show airing at 7.00 pm to be as safe for young viewers as a specifically targeted children's programme going out in the late afternoon. Peter Davison says he was untroubled by the violence within *Doctor Who*:

> I just do not buy the connection between screen violence and violence in society. I think it's a feeble excuse for the failings of society. It never bothered me at the time, I must admit. Call me irresponsible, it did not bother me. Yes, there was a high death count, but we're watching television and I think young people can distinguish

between television and reality. They're far more frightened by the news than they are by a television programme, a science fiction programme.[4]

Evidence does seem to be growing that there is at least some link between screen violence and violence in society. A number of studies have indicated a connection, but the results could equally be taken as evidence that violent young people are attracted to violent films, rather than showing that violent films produce violent people. The cause and effect are not necessarily clear. However, in February 2005 a report of a study at Birmingham University was published in *The Lancet* which confirmed a causal link – that is, screen violence *does* affect behaviour. But is such a study relevant to *Doctor Who*? The researchers say:

> There is consistent evidence that violent imagery in television, film and video, and computer games has substantial short-term effects on arousal, thoughts, and emotions, increasing the likelihood of aggressive or fearful behaviour in younger children, especially in boys.[5]

But, they say, the 'evidence becomes inconsistent' when looking at long-term effects or when considering older children. It is also worth noting that the material used in their research was much more violent than *Doctor Who* – films like *Saving Private Ryan*, *Kill Bill* and *Texas Chainsaw Massacre*. We all know *Doctor Who* can be scary, but its influence on violent behaviour is likely to be limited if films like these only produce 'a small but significant association'. A 15-year study in America revealed that the strongest effects came when children identified with the characters involved. The character we all identify with in *Doctor Who*, of course, is the Doctor himself – a champion of non-violence unless there really is no other option. He is hardly a model of aggressive behaviour, so the violence that is likely to most affect young viewers is that which the Doctor is on the receiving end of – and even on the very rare occasions when he is killed, he still quickly regenerates.

There is support for Davison's view that children can distinguish the fiction of television programmes from reality. A 2003 study showed that children find images of real-life violence much more disturbing than fictional ones. How they responded to the images was significantly affected by how realistic the images were, whether they felt the violence was justified and by its consequences.[6] The violence on *Doctor Who* is rarely graphic (though it became more so for a time and drew complaints from the National Viewers' and Listeners' Association) and almost never realistic. It is so far removed from normal life that even the youngest viewers are unlikely to be greatly disturbed by it – it's the menace of the Doctor's enemies (rather than their violence) that gives children nightmares. Nevertheless, the violence does often end with death, as Clayton Hickman, editor of *Doctor Who Magazine*, says:

> *Doctor Who* has always been a programme which has confronted death head on. From the very beginnings when the Daleks exterminated people they were dead. They weren't just slightly injured, they were gone.[7]

Another Way

The Doctor himself takes no pleasure in violence (let alone death) and does not seek it out, although it has a habit of finding him. His preferred approach is always to find non-violent means of sorting things out. One of the few times the Doctor seemed to be tempted to unnecessary violence came in the very first story, 'An Unearthly Child' (1963). While trying to escape from a tribe of stone-age humans, the Doctor and his companions are pursued by Za. When Za is subsequently attacked and wounded by a wild animal, the Doctor's companions try to help him. The Doctor believes that they are risking their own survival by this unnecessary kindness to an enemy, and he picks up a large, pointed stone, apparently to kill the unfortunate 'primitive' with. Ian restrains him, demanding an explanation. The Doctor hesitates, then claims he just wanted Za to draw a map of their route back to the TARDIS. Terrance Dicks says, 'It's quite obvious that he's thinking of polishing him off so they can get on with their escape. Now, you never had anything like that afterwards.'[8]

From then on, the Doctor's preference for avoiding violence was clear. Peter Davison says:

> He had a mission which was, I think, to appreciate the beautiful things in life. That's what he was trying to show. Violence is not necessary, you don't have to kill people. You can love a sunset and the smell of a flower.[9]

Or you can appreciate a jelly baby – and offer one to your enemy as the opening to an attempt at diplomacy. The fact that the Doctor tries for peaceful resolutions first is crucial in shaping the audience's feeling for him. Our respect for him is greater because his desire is to find a better way than force, yet he is prepared to use force when necessary. As we pointed out in Chapter 2, this makes him an unusual hero in science fiction or in any other action genre. Davison says:

> To me, he's your kind of anti-hero ... he's the hero but
> he's not the hero. He's not your gun-toting guy at all.[10]

Sylvester McCoy's Doctor is wonderfully heroic when he steps into the middle of a field of battle, armed with nothing more lethal than his umbrella, and commands the warring parties to stop ('Battlefield', 1989). Hartnell's Doctor is noble when he stays the hand of someone who is about to shoot a Dalek-enslaved Roboman after knocking him out. The Doctor insists calmly but firmly, 'No, Tyler, no. I never take life. Only when my own is immediately threatened' ('The Dalek Invasion of Earth', 1964). There is something wonderfully anti-heroic about someone with the capabilities of a Time Lord making himself a sonic screwdriver, although Captain Jack might have wished for something a little more deadly in 'The Doctor Dances'. Despite their discussion about the relative merits of guns, screwdrivers and bananas, the time does come when the Doctor needs Captain Jack's gun-toting expertise, but it would ruin our appreciation of the Doctor if this were what he was to become himself. When he searches for and finds a major weapon in Henry van Statten's underground facility so that he can destroy the Dalek, we understand why he's doing it, but there is also a sense of the Doctor going a little awry at this point. It's out of character.

Licence to Kill

Terrance Dicks comments that, 'He always tries for a peaceful resolution to any problem, but he never does it otherwise you get a boring show. But he does try.'[11] Dicks' implication that the show would be boring without the Doctor eventually being caught up in violence is an important one. Tension, conflict and resolution are at the heart of all good drama, but if diplomacy was always the solution to interstellar conflicts, *Doctor Who* would quickly lose its character as an action show, and it is hard to see how it would survive for long. With the Doctor's overriding concern to resolve crises and save those who are in danger, it is inevitable that the Doctor often finds himself in terrifying situations. Natural disasters, invasions, catastrophic accidents and brutal regimes have almost become the normal context in which to find him. As Clive says in 'Rose':

> The Doctor is a legend woven throughout history. When disaster comes, he's there. He brings a storm in his wake and he has one constant companion . . . death.

It is also inevitable that some of the monsters, despots, or other foes are not open to reason. There are always some who would rather kill the Doctor or some innocent beings than have anyone interfere with their plans for world or galactic domination. And so at times, even for the basically pacifist Doctor, it is kill or be killed, as when he shoots the leader of the Cybermen on board the TARDIS in 'Earthshock' (1982). But the need for killing is not often driven by the Doctor's instinct of self-preservation. Rather, it is because vulnerable beings need protecting against the violence which is being unleashed on them. He is prepared to kill a foe to prevent a much greater loss of life. 'Leave this planet,' he says to the Slitheen, 'or I'll kill you' ('World War Three'). This is the case every time the Doctor encounters the Daleks, and is part (though only part) of the Doctor's motivation for wanting to destroy what he believes is the last Dalek. He re-opens the bulkhead doors allowing the Dalek out for Rose's sake. But he also acts quickly to head it off and prevent the extermination of the million residents of nearby Salt Lake City.

While he doesn't relish the death of his enemies, there are times when he feels they deserve it. The Daleks are the most obvious example again – as we shall see later, the Doctor believes they are irredeemably evil. He also seems to believe that Margaret Slitheen deserves the death penalty she faces on her return to her home planet. Or at least, he considers her execution to be preferable to allowing her to continue wreaking havoc with innocent people's lives. As with the Dalek, he doesn't believe she can change, not in her case because of genetics, but because her evil patterns of behaviour are so deeply embedded. The TARDIS apparently shares the Doctor's fundamental aversion to death and enables Margaret to have a fresh start. Had that not happened, it is hard to imagine that the Doctor would not have kept to his plan to take her home. As Christopher Eccleston says:

> There's the other side to him, which is a ruthless, brutal pragmatist. If something or somebody is threatening the human race . . . he'll kill it.[12]

A more problematic example of the Doctor allowing the death of one of his foes is in 'The End of the World'. Having been exposed by the Doctor, Cassandra teleports away, taking her moisturising attendants with her. But the Doctor finds the hidden teleportation device and reverses it, returning her – but not the attendants – to Platform One. In the intense heat caused by her sabotage of the control systems, the 'bitchy trampoline' of stretched skin dries out rapidly. And with no one to moisturise Cassandra, the drying skin stretches tighter and tighter. It is unclear whether the Doctor foresaw this. As she cries, 'Have pity! Moisturise me! Oh Doctor!', Rose is horrified and asks the Doctor to help Cassandra. But it is too late and the Doctor tells Rose, 'Everything has its time and everything dies.' The Doctor was clearly an agent in Cassandra's death, but there is a sense in which he is not responsible for causing it. Cassandra had set out to murder every other guest on Platform One, with a degree of success. She had broken the law (not to mention the regulations about teleportation devices). It was right that she should be called to account for her actions instead of getting away with them. It is hardly the Doctor's fault if Cassandra's assistants did not return with her. Neither is it his fault that he had nothing to moisturise her with. It is entirely due to her own actions that the conditions on Platform One were so intolerable for her – both the actions which created the intense heat and the actions which made her so vulnerable to it. The Doctor simply facilitates her reaping what she herself had sown.

The Ultimate Sacrifice

Another problematic death is that of Gwyneth in 'The Unquiet Dead', whom the Doctor allows to die in order to stop the movement of the Gelth through the rift in time and space. Gwyneth is a good-hearted person who willingly offers herself to act as the bridge for the Gelth when she thinks they are in desperate need. Just as willingly, she strikes a match to destroy the building, the Gelth and herself after their true intentions are made clear. Rose thinks the Doctor is taking advantage of Gwyneth, although the maid insists that she knows her own mind. When she dies in the explosion, the Doctor informs Rose that Gwyneth was already dead and had been for some minutes, despite the apparent evidence to the contrary. The Doctor knows very well that there are times when people have to make the ultimate sacrifice in order to avert something much worse. Adric stowed away on the TARDIS after his brother Varsh sacrificed himself to save the Doctor and his friends ('Full Circle', 1980). He finally gave up his own life trying to break the navigational codes of a spaceship which the Cybermen had programmed to crash into the Earth and destroy it ('Earthshock', 1982). He failed, but had managed to take the freighter 65 million years back in time so it became the impact which killed the dinosaurs.

The Doctor is prepared to sacrifice himself too. He knows his value as a being of supreme intellect and with 900 years of experience in fighting evil, but he willingly risks – or gives up – his life for his friends, or for those he is seeking to protect. He risks his life leaping through the cooling fans on Platform One ('The End of the World'); he risks his life in getting a missile fired at 10 Downing Street where he is trapped with Rose and Harriet Jones. He gives his life twice in the 2005 series – once in an attempt to protect the wedding guests from the Reapers ('Father's Day'), and once to save Rose from the effects of the TARDIS' time vortex. On the former occasion the Doctor (along with the other Reaper victims) was restored to life through another act of self-sacrifice. Rose's dad, having seen the car that almost ran him down appear and disappear several times, concludes that the terrible events are happening because he did not die as he should have done. He says to Rose, 'I'm so useless I couldn't even die properly. Now it's my fault all this has happened.' It's not his fault at all, but he finally becomes the hero

Rose had always imagined him to be and goes outside to face his death.

When the Doctor saves Rose by kissing her and emptying the power of the time vortex from within her, it proves too much for him and he regenerates in spectacular style (standing up, for the first time). The Doctor regenerated after surrendering his life to save his companion once before. In 'The Caves of Adrozani' (1984), Peter Davison's Doctor and Peri are poisoned. He stumbles back to the TARDIS with Peri in his arms and carrying a vial of antidote. But as he fumbles for the TARDIS key he drops the vial and spills much of the precious liquid. Inside the TARDIS he pours the remaining antidote into Peri's mouth and lies down to die. Peri recovers quickly and is amazed to see the dying Doctor's transformation.

In Extremis

It is in these kinds of situations that *Doctor Who* shows us the very best and worst aspects of human life. On the one hand we see the capacity of an evil human (or monster[13]) to do enormous harm to others so that it can fulfil its evil desires. On the other hand, it is in extreme circumstances – whether in *Doctor Who* or in real life – that the very best of human nature shines through: integrity which is great enough not to break even under immense pressure, heart-rending compassion for those who are suffering, tremendous courage in the face of danger, and the measureless love of the ultimate self-sacrifice.

Death is the final reality for all of us. It's always an extreme situation, and it always tests the human heart – of those who die, those who are left, or both.

When the Doctor says to Rose after Cassandra's death,
'Everything has its time and everything dies', the tone
of his voice makes it clear that this is not the callous
or brutal expression that the words on the script might
otherwise suggest. It is a tone of resignation to the
grim realities of life. It is a view echoed in the book of
Ecclesiastes in the Bible:

> There is a time for everything,
> a season for every activity under heaven.
> A time to be born and a time to die.
> A time to plant and a time to harvest.
> A time to kill and a time to heal.
> A time to tear down and a time to rebuild.
> A time to cry and a time to laugh.
> A time to grieve and a time to dance.[14]

Ecclesiastes often touches on the inevitability of death,
and the apparent futility of life – in Chapter 2, for
example:

> I saw that wise and foolish people share the same fate.
> Both of them die ... and in the days to come, both will
> be forgotten.[15]

Cassandra's was a wasted life – a life of greed and
self-centredness, of hate and destruction. Her death
showed the folly of her life – there was no sense of
the world being a better place for her having been in
it, rather the reverse. It need not be so. American poet
and undertaker Thomas Lynch writes:

> The figure most often and most conspicuously missing
> from the insurance charts and demographics is the one I
> call THE BIG ONE, which refers to the number of people
> out of every hundred born who will die ... it is a useful

number and has its lessons. Maybe you will want to figure out what to do with your life. Maybe it will make you feel a certain kinship with the rest of us. Maybe it will make you hysterical.[16]

In 'The Dalek Invasion of Earth' (1964), Jenny, one of the human rebels, reflects on their wheelchair-bound leader having just gone to throw bombs at the Daleks. She says to the Doctor's companion Barbara, 'There is nothing heroic about dying! There's no point in throwing lives away just to prove a principle.' Barbara replies, 'If Dortmun hadn't thrown his life away we would all be dead. He knew exactly what he was doing. He sacrificed himself so that you and I would have a chance.' A life given to save others is certainly not a life wasted.

Cheating Death

And yet, while death is inevitable, and despite the possibility of both our lives and our deaths achieving something of value, most people still fear it, sometimes going to great lengths to try to avoid or postpone it. That is, of course, why the scenes at the end of 'The Doctor Dances' are so deeply moving: 'Oh come on, give me a day like this,' murmurs the Doctor as he watches the nanogenes cluster around Jamie and Nancy. 'Give me this one!' And then, moments later after the Doctor has dispersed the nanogenes to the other empty people, he exclaims, 'Everybody lives, Rose! Just this once, everybody lives!' Surely this is one of the most uplifting moments in the entire history of *Doctor Who*. Death has been cheated – for a while. Rose's reversal of the deaths caused by the Daleks ('Parting of the Ways') is also extraordinary. Perhaps too much so, as a number of fans feel that this *deus ex machina*[17] is too simple a way of sorting things out and bringing the series to an end. It is likely to be hotly debated among fans for a long time to come.

The Doctor's regenerations are, of course, a fabulous way of cheating death – the possibility of something of a fresh start, yet also some continuity with what has gone before. It has often been said in *Doctor Who* that Time Lords are limited to twelve regenerations (first revealed in 'The Deadly Assassin', 1976). But there have also been contradictions. The Master was offered an extra set of regenerations in 'The Five Doctors' (1983) and Rassilon apparently discovered the secret of perpetual regeneration, so maybe the Doctor could go on for more than three more incarnations after David Tennant.

The Final Victory

The Doctor's regeneration is, up to a point, an interesting parallel with the Christian belief in the resurrection of God's Son Jesus Christ after he had been killed on a Roman cross. This is not the place to go into a detailed defence of the evidence for this,[18] nor into a detailed explanation of all of the theological implications. But it is worth setting out briefly how the Christian view of death and resurrection compares with the views on death within *Doctor Who*.

The biblical perspective on death is that it is inevitable, as we saw from Ecclesiastes. It will happen sooner or later. But in a marked difference from most deaths in *Doctor Who*, death for the Christian is not the end. *Doctor Who* almost always assumes that the 'soul' of a person[19] is extinguished at death; there is nothing more to life because we are entirely physical beings without 'souls'. But Christians believe that humans are both physical and spiritual.[20] Therefore we can die in two ways – physically and spiritually. Physical death is obvious; spiritual death less so, but it is no less real. Spiritual death is being disconnected from God and the life that is found in him. It is a consequence of the human race's rebellion against God, breaking the relationship with him that we were created for. Physical death means the end of our lives in these bodies on this Earth – a problem humans try to postpone for as long as possible. Spiritual death means being cut off from God for eternity – a far more serious problem which many people give little thought to.

The answer to this problem has echoes in a number of *Doctor Who* stories – one life being given up in order to save many lives. The Christian conviction is that Jesus of Nazareth was God born in human form – fully God and fully human at the same time. He was also the only human never to rebel against God in even the slightest degree. This qualified him to offer himself as a sacrifice on behalf of all humanity. An illustration of this is the Doctor's sacrifice in 'Parting of the Ways'. As the Doctor takes into his own body the deadly effects of Rose's encounter with the TARDIS' time vortex, so that he will die instead of her, so Jesus takes the consequences of our rebellion against God (which the Bible refers to as sin) on himself and dies in our place.[21] We will still have to face physical death one day, but if we accept that this sacrifice was made on our behalf we become alive spiritually forever – an eternity in relationship with God.[22]

However, Christians also believe that since Jesus was more than just a human, because he was also God, it was impossible for death to keep its hold on him. Like the Doctor, he is too powerful for death to defeat. By contrast, while the Doctor only puts off death until he finally comes to the end of his twelve regenerations, Jesus will never have to go through death again, because death has been conclusively defeated, not just cheated for a while. God raised Jesus from the dead, and this resurrection is a confirmation from God that those who put their trust in Jesus will also be raised to eternal life. Humanity's great enemy death will have been finally and utterly destroyed.[23]

Inescapable Death

Doctor Who treads a fine line between the Doctor's admirably non-violent principles and the reality of death as an inescapable part of our existence. The fact that the show doesn't shy away from confronting the issue head on is arguably one of the things that has given it such enduring appeal. This isn't a cosy imaginary world without threat or danger, it is a universe red in tooth and claw, where our worst fears have to be confronted. And of course, the Doctor does confront them, and he always wins (although rarely without casualties along the way). But in the final analysis, the Doctor is only ever able to delay the inevitable. For all our joy at the climax to 'The Doctor Dances', the multitude who are saved from oblivion will one day face death again. For a permanent solution we must look elsewhere.

Notes

[1] Russell T. Davies, *Doctor Who Confidential: The Daleks* (BBC3, first broadcast 30 April 2005).

2   Peter Davison, *Doctor Who Confidential: The Daleks.*

3   Russell T. Davies, *Doctor Who Confidential: The Daleks.*

4   Peter Davison, *Doctor Who Confidential: The Daleks.*

5   Kevin Browne and Catherine Hamilton-Giachritsis, 'The influence of violent media on children and adolescents: a public-health approach', *The Lancet,* Volume 365, Number 9460, 19 February 2005.

6   Andrea Millwood Hargrave, *How Children Interpret Screen Violence,* BBC, British Board of Film Classification, Broadcasting Standards Commission, Independent Television Commission, September 2003 – available from www.ofcom.org.uk.

7   Clayton Hickman, *Doctor Who Confidential: The Daleks.*

8   Terrance Dicks, *The Story of Doctor Who* (BBC2, first broadcast as part of '*Doctor Who* Night', Saturday 19 March 2005).

9   Peter Davison, *Doctor Who Confidential: Why On Earth?* (BBC3, first broadcast 23 April 2005).

10 Peter Davison, *The Story of Doctor Who.*

11 Terrance Dicks, *The Story of Doctor Who.*

12 Christopher Eccleston, *Doctor Who Confidential: Why On Earth?*

13 But as we argue in Chapter 7, these monsters do reflect aspects of our own human nature.

14 Ecc. 3:1–4, New Living Translation.

15 Ecc. 2:14–16, NLT.

16 Thomas Lynch, *The Undertaking* (Vintage, 1998), p. 4–5.

17 *deus ex machina* (literally: god out of the machine) an unlikely plot device to bring about a simple resolution to a dramatic crisis. The origin of the phrase is in ancient Greek and Roman theatre, which sometimes introduced one of the gods (played by an actor suspended above the stage by a machine) to tie all the loose plot ends together.

18 cf. William Lane Craig, 'Contemporary Scholarship and the Historical Evidence for the Resurrection of Jesus Christ' at www.leaderu.com/truth/1truth22.html; or William Lane Craig, *The Son Rises,* (Wipf & Stock, 2001).

[19] The word 'soul' here is not meant in an explicitly religious sense, but more in the sense of human consciousness.

[20] cf. William Hasker, *The Emergent Self* (Cornell University Press, 2001); J.P. Moreland, *Scaling the Secular City*, (Baker, 1987); Victor Reppert, *C.S. Lewis's Dangerous Idea* (IVP, 2003); Richard Swinburne, *The Evolution of the Soul*, (Clarendon Press, 1997); Charles Taliaferro, *Consciousness and the Mind of God* (Cambridge, 2005).

[21] Not that this analogy suggests that looking into the time vortex is the equivalent of rebellion against God, in the sense of being a bad thing, merely that the consequences of the action brought death.

[22] cf. Alister McGrath, *What Was God Doing On The Cross?* (Wipf & Stock, 2002).

[23] cf. Gary R. Habermas & J.P. Moreland, *Beyond Death* (Good News, 1998).

7. Terrors From the Deep

She's not even a she, she's a thing
Mickey in 'Boom Town'

The second *Doctor Who* story in 1963 established monsters as a crucial factor in the appeal and success of the show. However, just because monsters (bug-eyed or otherwise) feature so heavily in *Doctor Who*, that doesn't mean that Sidney Newman's worst fears of slack-jawed mindless horror and cheap thrills for the viewers came to pass. The best *Doctor Who* monsters are more subtle and significant than that.

Demonstrative Monsters

'Science fiction is peerless as a framing device for our concerns.'

Matt Hanson[1]

There is an important distinction to be made in *Doctor Who* between aliens and monsters. We have already seen in Chapter 5 that it would be unfair to describe Jabe as a monster, despite her alien nature. She is clearly on the Doctor's side and nobly sacrifices herself for the common good. In general terms, we may define a monster as any scary entity, whether that be a human who looks no different to anyone else but who is monstrous in a moral sense (such as Adolf Hitler or Henry van Statten), or an alien creature whose nature represents a threat. But if we are to understand the role that monsters play in *Doctor Who* (other than that of plot device) we need a wider understanding of their role in society.

According to Nick Capasso, monsters are everywhere, and always have been:

> These terrible and wonderful beings, since the dawn of human consciousness, have lurked at the edges and stood front and centre in all our far-flung cultures. Their ubiquity and longevity are based on their power and adaptability as symbols and metaphors for a great number of things, all centred upon anxiety.[2]

The word 'monster' can be traced to various Latin roots related to education. The Latin *monstrum* means 'that which teaches', while *monstrare* means 'to show'. Both words derive from *monere*, meaning 'to warn'. This theme of teaching, showing or warning is obvious from the related English word 'demonstrate'. The Latin *demonstratum* is a past participle of *demonstrare*, and means: 'to point out, indicate, show or prove'.[3] So the role of the monster is to show us something, to warn and to teach us.

According to Capasso: 'monsters can and do pack powerful emotional and psychological wallops. Our primal fears have not gone away, and the monster remains the most effective tool for visualizing and confronting them.'[4] For example, the Mandrels in 'Nightmare of Eden' (1979) were, quite literally, an anti-social drug on legs! Imaginary monsters exist as ways of confronting real or possible evils. The more monstrous the evil, and the more successfully the monster symbolises that evil, the scarier it is. In this way, monsters often fulfil a prophetic role in society, showing and warning us about uncomfortable truths. Stories like *Doctor Who*, in which symbolic monsters are defeated, work as 'a drama of reassurance',[5] suggesting that our deepest fears and anxieties can be overcome and conquered.

As society changes, so new sources of anxiety are born, and new monsters are created which tap in to these new fears. For example, the Autons who terrorised Rose in her first encounter with the Doctor had previously featured in two adventures from the Pertwee era. Writer Robert Holmes had noted the presence of plastic as a new material that was becoming common in British life in the late 1960s, and invented the plastic-manipulating Nestene Consciousness as a way of representing concerns about how this wonder-material might affect British life.

Genesis of the Daleks

The real life genesis of the Daleks was sparked by comedian Tony Hancock and given finesse by a troupe of dancers. Writer Terry Nation spent some time touring with Hancock after his split from writers Ray Galton and Alan Simpson. (Hancock never used Nation's material. He reverted to routines from the 1950s when on stage and Nation ended up being Hancock's minder.) They shared a room on the tour, and would stay up half the night debating the fate of mankind. The ever-paranoid Hancock believed that humanity would be wiped out and was fascinated by the question of what form of life, if any, would survive. Hancock's obsession led Nation to write a story about a race so mutated and devastated by war that they were forced to encase themselves in armoured travelling machines in order to go about their business.

Much of the impact of the Daleks was based on the fact that nothing like them had ever been seen before. Here were aliens who did *not* look like a man in a rubber mask, an effect achieved by designing a non-human shell around a seated human operator.

Terry Nation's instructions to designer Ray Cusick were to give the Daleks smooth flowing movements, based on a television performance Nation had seen by the Georgian State Dancers. The comparison fired Cusick's imagination, and he swiftly developed what we now recognise as the classic Dalek design, replacing the Georgians' hooped, foot-hiding skirts with a metallic lower section. Wheels under the casing enabled the creatures to glide effortlessly along the floor, much as the dancers had appeared to float when dancing. The clawed appendages called for in Nation's script were replaced with the sucker and gun combination that we know today. More significantly, the Daleks were made slightly smaller than average human height, giving the viewer pause to question whether or not there really was a human operator inside. For whatever reason, the image worked, and viewers were instantly fascinated by the latest addition to the pantheon of science fiction monsters.

However, the power of the Daleks was not just a matter of great design work. It was a matter of their symbolic meaning. The depiction of the Dalek's planet of Skaro as one devastated by atomic war came only a year after the Cuban missile crisis of 1962; while 1964's 'The Dalek Invasion of Earth' symbolically depicted the

Nazi invasion of Britain many viewers had feared two decades before:

> It is all too easy to watch the Daleks and to see them merely as successful science-fiction monsters. But ... their real impact was that they showed us what our own fate might one day be – or even, by paralleling relatively recent events in Germany, what the human race had already become.[6]

Subsequent Dalek stories have continued to add layers of meaning to the monstrous Daleks, endowing them with up-to-date significance. In the 1970s the character of Davros was introduced to re-explain the Dalek's origins in terms of genetic engineering – an extension of the eugenic concerns of their Nazi role models. In 2005, Russell T. Davies turned the Daleks into a bunch of religious fundamentalists, blindly worshipping their 'God' (the re-introduced Emperor Dalek), issuing threatening commands not to blaspheme, and portraying their enemy (the Doctor) as the great Satan. This new departure for the Daleks has to be understood in the context of the raised level of concern about Islamic terrorism and the 'war on terror' that was declared by George W. Bush in the light of attack on the World Trade Centre on 11 September 2001. We will explore the attitude of *Doctor Who* to religion at greater length in Chapter 9.

Tampering with Nature

Since the 1960s, advances in scientific knowledge and medical technology have raised the question of how much we can tamper with ourselves before we cease to be human. *Doctor Who* frequently draws upon this theme, turning fears about losing our humanity into Daleks, Cybermen and Sontarans:

> Daleks, Cybermen and Sontarans, notorious *Doctor Who* monsters, threaten not just extermination, but a 'post-human' catastrophe: the collapse of our essential humanity ... Unlike other monsters, which simply attack externally, Daleks and Cybermen (Cyborgs) and Sontarans (clones) present an additional chilling threat: that we might become like them, and become the monsters they are.[7]

Having re-introduced Daleks in the 2005 series of *Doctor Who*, it comes as no surprise to learn that Cybermen (precursors to *Star Trek: the Next Generation*'s Borg[8]) will be returning to *Doctor Who* in 2006.

In the 1970s environmental concerns became a part of popular consciousness, and *Doctor Who* turned these anxieties into a series of monsters designed to highlight concerns over green issues. For example, the Sea Devils and the Silurians were both intelligent reptilian creatures that threatened to pay humanity back for causing their near extinction. In 'The Green Death' (1973) the Doctor faced a plague of giant maggots inadvertently created by the dumping of industrial waste into a disused Welsh mine. The Slitheen family represent every corporation that treats the planet as a moneymaking resource without regard for the collateral damage caused by their operations.

Beyond Good and Evil

Richard Ebbs insightfully comments that, 'generally we find that the monsters who evoke such fear and fascination in us represent aspects of ourselves, and since we fear them, a conflict must therefore exist within ourselves.'[9] He argues that, where what he calls 'dualist' religious views are accepted, a war ensues between an individual's conscious mind and subconscious aspects of the self. He says that if any aspect of the self is in conflict with the conscious mind, it acquires a demonic, or monster-like appearance. Ebbs sees this conflict as an 'illusion fostered by the conscious mind itself.'[10] He concludes that:

> In a world where there is no absolute good or absolute evil, and where all things (i.e. the 'inner' and the 'outer') are connected, then the practice of forging alliances with our monsters and demons, where possible, has the potential to increase our awareness, and help us to become more integrated human beings.[11]

Ebbs assumes that 'there is no absolute good or absolute evil', but he also assumes that to 'increase our awareness' and to become 'more integrated human beings' are *good* things! Thus his position appears to be self-contradictory. If Ebbs is wrong about the non-reality of good and evil,[12] his advice may achieve the elimination of inner conflict with our personal demons at the risk of becoming, like the Daleks, 'creatures without conscience, no sense of right or wrong'.[13]

What Ebbs ignores in his account of 'dualist' religion, is that while it recognises and so highlights the conflict between good and evil within humanity, it can also promise an *eventual* resolution of that conflict, where good ultimately triumphs over evil. For now, however, Ebbs' path to monster elimination is also a path to the elimination of the monster's nemesis, the hero. A world without good or evil is as much a world without heroes as it is a world without monsters. Further implications of this way of thinking are revealed by returning – as *Doctor Who* does so often – to the Daleks.

Davros

Doctor: The Dalek race was genetically engineered. Every
   single emotion was removed, except hate.
van Statten: Genetically engineered! By whom?
Doctor: By a genius, van Statten. By a man who was king of
   his own little world. You'd like him.

('Dalek')

As we discovered in 'Genesis of the Daleks' (1975), the
creation of the Doctor's greatest foes was the work of
the greatest scientist of the Kaled race, a mutant named
Davros. Having realised that the mutation of the Kaleds
was unstoppable, Davros conducted experiments to
determine his people's final mutational form and
devised a 'travel machine' to ensure their survival.

Davros is a scientific Hitler to the Daleks' SS shock
troops. At Auschwitz, Hitler's words reveal how he
'freed Germany from the stupid and degrading fallacies
of conscience and morality ... I want people capable
of violence – imperious, ruthless and cruel.'[14] Davros
echoes Hitler's ideology, working to create a master-
race 'utterly devoid of conscience'. Davros talks of
creating 'the supreme creature, the ultimate conqueror
of the universe, the Dalek', and describes the Doctor's
conscience as his greatest weakness.

The Daleks lack conscience by design: 'Davros has
one of the finest scientific minds in existence,' observes
the Doctor, 'but he has a fanatical desire to perpetuate
himself and his machines, he works without conscience,
without soul, and without pity, and his machines are
equally devoid of these qualities.' Rob Shearman,
writer of 'Dalek', reveals: 'I always see [Daleks] as
evil children who don't have any morals yet, and will
connive any way they can to get what they want.'[15]
Hence the Daleks not only represent the historical evils

of Nazism and nuclear war, but the capacity for evil inherent in each and every human being.

Daleks remind us that scientific knowledge purchases power but not wisdom. They remind us that science detached from conscience may lead to disaster. George Gilder and Jay W. Richards ask: 'What will happen when our technological achievements give us Promethean powers – powers once thought the exclusive province of God – just when most of those in charge have ceased to believe in anyone or anything like God?'[16] The Daleks are a prophetic response to this question, warning us that altering nature, especially our own nature, isn't necessarily a good thing. As G.K. Chesterton (no relation to Ian, as far as we are aware) warned:

> When once one begins to think of man as a shifting and alterable thing, it is always easy for the strong and crafty to twist him into new shapes for all kinds of unnatural purposes ... Whatever wild image one employs it cannot keep pace with the panic of the human fancy, when once it supposes that the fixed type called man could be changed ... That is the nightmare with which the mere notion of adaption threatens us. This is the nightmare that is not so very far from the reality. It will be said that not the wildest evolutionist really asks that we should become in any way unhuman ... Pardon me, but this is exactly what not merely the wildest evolutionists urge, but some of the tamest evolutionists, too.[17]

Taking Stock of Genetic Engineering

Davros is as wild an evolutionist as one could hope not to meet. By contrast, Gregory Stock is a tame evolutionist, Director of the Program on Medicine, Technology and Society at the School of Medicine at UCLA. His book, *Redesigning Humans – choosing our children's genes* (Profile Books, 2002), advocates consciously designing future generations. Stock takes his atheistic assumption to its logical conclusion and denies that human nature is in any way 'sacred', or that 'playing God' with human nature is a problem. Stock embraces genetic engineering despite his belief that we 'cannot know where self-directed evolution will take us, nor hope to control the process for very long.'[18]

Stock believes that humans are the outcome of an unintended evolutionary process who, having developed the power to take over their own evolution where nature left off, should direct it towards 'the goals we value'.[19] The question of whether those goals are good ones doesn't seem to occur to him. Neither does the issue of what kind of universe we must live in if goals can be good. However, as philosopher Winfried Corduan explains, the non-theist who believes that there are things that we objectively *ought* to value, 'is after an obligatory moral code without anything that makes it obligatory. To have commandments, they must be commanded in some way, but the atheist's system does not allow for such a possibility.'[20]

Stock admits that genetic engineering 'would replace the hand of an all-knowing and almighty creator with our own clumsy fingers and instruments', and thereby 'trade the cautious pace of natural evolutionary change for the careless speed of high technology ... flying forward with no idea where we were going and no safety net to catch us',[21] but for him there is no creator to worry about or replace. Like the Emperor Dalek, Stock thinks that we can play at being God with impunity. There is no God with a good purpose behind our existence to usurp. We must simply do our best to channel our conquest of nature: 'If ... we admit that we don't know where we are headed, maybe we will

work harder to ensure that the process itself serves us
... that is what we must count on.'[22] Ironically, Stock
begins one of his chapters with the following quotation
from Lewis Carroll's *Alice in Wonderland*:

> 'Cheshire Puss,' she began ... 'would you tell me, please,
> which way I ought to go from here?' 'That depends a
> good deal on where you want to get to,' said the Cat.
> 'I don't much care where,' said Alice. 'Then it doesn't
> matter which way you go,' said the Cat.'

The Extermination of Man

In his brief but seminal book *The Abolition of Man*,
C.S. Lewis observes that what we call man's power is
in fact power possessed by some men by which they
may or may not allow others to profit. Each new power
won by man is also a power over man. The ultimate
stage in man's conquest of nature, and so of men's
power over mankind, says Lewis, will come when man
has obtained the power to control himself. What would
happen if this power were used without reference to a
belief in objective good and evil?

Lewis points out that in the traditional system of
education, teachers believed in an objective set of
moral values, which they served by seeking to produce
people who also conformed to those values. But if
humanity rejects this concept, preferring a subjective
approach to morality, then how will we determine
what kind of person educators are looking to produce?
When there is no right and wrong, what basis is there
for not producing moral monsters like the Daleks? The
conditioners will choose what moral opinions they will
produce in humans (just as Davros chooses to condition
the Daleks 'simply to survive ... by becoming the

dominant species'), but by ignoring the moral law, the conditioners will have stepped into the void. Lewis goes on to say that this process does not produce men, but artefacts: man-made things as lacking in humanity as the luckless Jamie in 'The Empty Child'. Where no objective values exist there can be no basis for doing anything, other than the strength of one emotional impulse over another. Just as the Jamie/gas mask hybrid could do nothing but search desperately for its mother, so humanity sets foot on a path that leads only to slavery to our primal instincts.

At the moment of our supposed conquest of nature, we may find humanity in general subjected to a few individuals, and those individuals subjected to their irrational, 'natural' impulses. Hence, in 'Parting of the Ways' we meet an Emperor Dalek who, having been sent mad by the Time War, declares itself to be a god and creates a new race of equally mad Daleks in its own perverted image.

Burning Fear

As a result of Davros' genetic programming Daleks are the ultimate xenophobes – hating all other races simply because they are different. As the Doctor explains in 'Dalek': 'If the Dalek gets out it will murder every living creature ... because it honestly believes they should die. Human beings are different, and anything different is wrong. It is the ultimate in racial cleansing.'

The implacable Daleks may be the most frightening monsters in the *Doctor Who* universe, but in a world where everything else is 'wrong', they may also be the most frightened. As Christopher Eccleston insightfully comments: 'This great, cold steel instrument of destruction, all that casing, all that armour, is actually to protect this very vulnerable, strange, frightened creature.'[23] In 'Parting of the Ways', the Doctor exposes and plays upon the Daleks' buried fear: 'You might have removed all your emotions, but I reckon right down deep in your DNA there's one little spark left, and that's fear. Doesn't it just burn when you face me?'

Davros is ruled by a 'fanatical desire to perpetuate himself', a desire that therefore rules over his creatures to such an extent that they are the ultimate social Darwinians. Daleks are consumed by a need to exterminate all non-conformity, unless it is useful for their all-consuming goal of becoming the supreme beings of the universe. Likewise, Lewis warns that nature will rule the conditioners, and through them, humanity:

> Either we are ... obliged for ever to obey the absolute value ... or else we are mere nature to be kneaded and cut into new shapes for the pleasures of masters who must, by hypothesis, have no motive but their own 'natural' impulses ... A dogmatic belief in objective values is necessary to the very idea of a rule which is not tyranny or an obedience which is not slavery.[24]

Stock's Self-Abolition

'It couldn't kill van Statten, it couldn't kill me – it's changing. What about you Doctor? What the hell are you changing into?'

(Rose, in 'Dalek')

Stock admits that since 'We cannot know where self-directed evolution will take us, nor hope to control the process for very long',[25] this process will lead to the extermination of the 'we' that it is meant to serve, as nobody will want to be left behind: 'future generations will not want to remain "natural" if that means living at the whim of *advanced creatures to whom they would be little more than interesting relics from an abandoned human past.*'[26] Stock also acknowledges that: 'In offering ourselves as vessels for potential transformation into we know not what, we are submitting to the shaping hand of a process that dwarfs us individually.'[27] The process Stock wants us to embrace on the basis of its *benefits to us* in enhancing *our* nature actually dwarfs its supposed controllers in such a way that they will be swallowed up by the process they initiate. Furthermore, in rejecting God, man rejects any objective basis for thinking that the proposed enhancements are an objectively good thing in the first place! The whole project is self-contradictory and self-defeating. Lewis describes this as the 'magician's bargain' – to give up our souls in return for power. The flaw in this Faustian pact is that once we give up our souls, none of the power belongs to us. Once we treat ourselves as raw material, raw material is all that we will be.

To resist genetic engineering of the type employed by Davros to create the Daleks we must be able to say that there is an inherent dignity and worth in human nature, and that it is objectively true that this should not be abolished. Such a statement is only possible in a theistic worldview.[28] As Stock asks, 'where does this "right" [to an unaltered genetic constitution] come from? The assertion is spiritual, and virtually identical to the declaration that we should not play God. One cannot rebut this as a religious belief, but it is unconvincing in secular garb.'[29]

Daleks rank among the all-time great monsters because they represent the worst of humanity's past (Nazism, nuclear war) *and* threaten a 'post-human' catastrophe.

They neither look nor sound human, and yet they were once humanoid. More than that, stories such as 'Bad Wolf'/'Parting of the Ways' have the Daleks assimilating humans and transforming them into Daleks, tapping into our anxieties about losing our own humanity. The origins of the Daleks are a warning against embracing the power of science without the wisdom of morality. A Dalek is a genius that 'can calculate a thousand billion combinations in one second flat', but that doesn't mean that it makes right decisions in life.

Moral Monsters

There is a moral monstrosity in humanity that the monsters we invent represent; a moral monstrosity that demands to be acknowledged and opposed. To deny the reality of evil is to exterminate both the concept of heroism and any possibility of a principled opposition to those asking us to welcome the 'post human condition' that some of the scariest monsters in *Doctor Who* warn us against.

In the 2005 version of *Doctor Who* it is the human characters who are actually the most evil. Consider Cassandra's profit-motivated callous scheming ('The End of the World'), Henry van Statten's casual willingness to mind-wipe his assistants and to torture his captive 'Metaltron' ('Dalek'); the Editor's collaboration in mankind's slavery and Adam's desire to get rich quick ('The Long Game'). All of these people had a choice. Gas mask people can't help rewriting the DNA of everyone they touch, and nobody (even Jack) can really be blamed for their actions; Daleks can't help being homicidal, but Davros chose to make them that way. He is responsible.

Moral evil exists because those who have the freedom to choose make choices they ought not to make. As the Doctor says of his fellow Time Lords in 'Trial of a Time Lord' (1986): 'The oldest civilization: decadent, degenerate, and rotten to the core . . . Daleks, Sontarans . . . Cybermen, they're still in the nursery compared to us. Ten million years of absolute power. That's what it takes to be really corrupt.' A monster is a human invention that warns us about our own capacity for evil and demonstrates our need to be saved from ourselves. The 'dualist' worldview of the Bible has an absolutely good transcendent creator involving himself in human history, offering forgiveness and promising the eventual triumph of good over evil. This fits the evidence of morality (evil is real), and means that the human story is ultimately, like *Doctor Who*, a drama of reassurance.

Notes

1   Matt Hanson, *Building Sci-Fi Moviescapes* (Rotovision, 2004), p. 8.
2   Nick Capasso, 'Monsters Everywhere and Forever' at www.decordova.org/decordova/exhibit/terrors/essays. htm
3   cf. Richard Ebbs, 'Monsters' at www.feedback.nildram. co.uk/richardebbs/essays/monsters.htm
4   Capasso, 'Monsters Everywhere and Forever'.
5   John Tullock, *Science Fiction Audiences* (Routledge, 1995), p. 61.
6   Justin Richards, *Doctor Who: The Legend* (BBC, 2003), p. 12.
7   Anthony Thacker, *A Closer Look At Science Fiction* (Kingsway, 2001), p. 163.
8   The Borg are a cybernetic race, whose aim is to incorporate all intelligent life forms into their collective consciousness.

The chief distinctions between the two monsters are that the Cybermen do not have a collective consciousness, and the Borg generally have sexier outfits.

9   Richard Ebbs, 'Monsters'.

10 Richard Ebbs, 'Monsters'.

11 Richard Ebbs, 'Monsters'.

12 On the objectivity of good and evil cf. Peter Kreeft, 'A Refutation of Moral Relativism' at www.peterkreeft.com/audio/05_relativism.htm (Audio File); Francis J. Beckwith & Gregory Koukl, *Relativism: Feet Firmly Planted in Mid-Air* (Baker, 1998).

13 Garman, 'Genesis of the Daleks' (1975).

14 Quoted by Ravi Zacharias, *Can Man Live Without God?*, (Word, 1995), p. 68.

15 Robert Shearman, *Radio Times*, 30 April–6 May 2005, p. 20.

16 George Gilder and Jay W. Richards, 'Are We Spiritual Machines?' in Jay W. Richards (ed.) *Are We Spiritual Machines? Ray Kurzweil vs. The Critics of Strong AI*, (Discovery Institute, 2002), p. 8.

17 G.K. Chesterton, *What's Wrong With The World*, (Dodd, Mead and Company, 1910, reprinted Ignatius, 1994), p. 180–181.

18 Gregory Stock, *Redesigning Humans* (Profile, 2002), p. 173.

19 Gregory Stock, *Redesigning Humans*, p. 201.

20 Winfried Corduan, *No Doubt about It* (College Press), p. 87.

21 Gregory Stock, *Redesigning Humans*, p. 175.

22 Gregory Stock, *Redesigning Humans*, p. 175.

23 Christopher Eccleston, 'Time for a change, says new Dr Who', *The Daily Telegraph*, Thursday, 29 April, 2005.

24 C.S. Lewis, *The Abolition of Man* (Fount, 1999) or at www.columbia.edu/cu/augustine/arch/lewis/abolition1.htm#1.

25 Gregory Stock, *Redesigning Humans*, p. 173.

26 Gregory Stock, *Redesigning Humans*, p. 199, our italics.

27 Gregory Stock, *Redesigning Humans*, p. 173.

28 cf. William Lane Craig, 'The Indispensability of Theological

Meta-Ethical Foundations for Morality' at www.leaderu. com/offices/billcraig/docs/meta-eth.html.
[29] Gregory Stock, *Redesigning Humans*, p. 129.

8. More To Learn

And with that sentence you've just lost the right to even talk to me.

The Doctor in 'Bad Wolf'

No human failing annoys the Doctor more than having a closed mind. He berates Charles Dickens for having 'one of the best minds in the world' yet failing to accept what he had plainly seen when the gaseous Gelth showed themselves ('The Unquiet Dead'). Later, when Dickens refuses to take part in a séance, the Doctor has to encourage him to think again, saying, 'Humbug? Come on – open mind!' But the great writer isn't there yet. He has prided himself on his scepticism concerning paranormal activity (which he refers to as 'illusions', 'cheap mummery' and 'the work of fantasists') but is in fact as resistant to the truth as some of those he has sought to 'unmask'. The curious contradiction within Dickens at this point is not really explored. Self-styled 'sceptics' frequently present themselves as 'free thinkers' who don't accept religious or paranormal ideas and experiences at face value, trying to find explanations which exclude the supernatural. This is exemplified by the Charles Dickens we meet at the beginning of this episode – a 'free-thinker' who refuses to think freely, who refuses to countenance the idea that there could be something beyond what he already knows.

Time and again the Doctor has struggled with the obstinacy, pettiness, selfishness and stupidity of closed minds. In 'Paradise Towers' (1987), Sylvester McCoy's Doctor finds himself in a giant, decaying tower block, the inhabitants of which are busy fighting each other while a megalomaniac caretaker tries to destroy them all. The challenge for the Doctor is to persuade the factions to look beyond their differences and see the common enemy. Very often it is closed-minded humans refusing to accept what the Doctor says who hamper his efforts and get people killed. In 'Dalek', the Doctor tries to help van Statten's soldiers in their battle with the Dalek, only for his advice to be rebuffed with a dismissive, 'Thank you Doctor, but I think I know how to fight one single tin robot.' The carnage that follows is an eloquent proof that the officer's confidence was misplaced.

Different is Wrong

Closed minds are, like stagnant ponds, liable to give rise to other unpleasant characteristics. The most obvious of these is intolerance. The Doctor has met many deeply intolerant beings in his time. The essence of every evil genius is either greed or hate, or both. The greedy are often just careless of others' lives, but the hateful are driven by intolerance, none more so than the Daleks. Just how intolerant they are, the Doctor makes clear to Henry van Statten:

> *van Statten*: I thought you were the great expert, Doctor. If you're so impressive, then why not just reason with this Dalek? It must be willing to negotiate. There must be something it needs – everything needs something.

Doctor: Where's the nearest town?
van Statten: Salt Lake City.
Doctor: Population?
van Statten: One million.
Doctor: All dead. If the Dalek gets out it will murder every living creature. That's all it needs.
van Statten: But why would it *do* that?
Doctor: Because it honestly believes they should die. Human beings are different, and anything different is wrong. It's the ultimate in racial cleansing. And you, van Statten, you've let it loose!

The Daleks have always been extreme fascists – 'the alien equivalent of Nazis'.[1] So strong is their hatred of anything different from themselves that when a group of renegade Daleks vies with the Imperial Daleks to find the Hand of Omega ('Remembrance of the Daleks', 1988), they want to destroy each other, as Ace explains:

Renegade Daleks are blobs. Imperial Daleks are bionic blobs with bits added. You can tell that Daleks are into racial purity. One lot of Daleks reckon the other lot of blobs are too different. They're mutants. Not pure in their 'blobbiness' . . . They hate each other's chromosomes – war to the death.

Russell T. Davies gives an interesting new twist to the Daleks at the end of the 2005 series. Reflecting the concerns of today's world rather than old fears of Nazi fascism, he turns them into religious fundamentalists ('Parting of the Ways'). The Emperor Dalek tells the Doctor that in order to rebuild his army, the Daleks have harvested 'the waste of humanity. The prisoners, the refugees, the dispossessed – they all came to us. The bodies were filleted, pulped, sifted. The seed of the human race is perverted; only one cell in a billion is fit to be nurtured.' Rose comments that the new Dalek army must be half-human, and is shouted down by Daleks accusing her of blasphemy. This prompts the Doctor to ask, 'Since when did the Daleks have a concept of blasphemy?' In reply, the Emperor echoes and parodies the God of the Bible, saying, 'I reached into the dirt and made new life. I am the god of all Daleks!' His followers chorus, 'Worship him!' and the Doctor comments, 'They're insane! Hiding in the silence for hundreds of years, that's enough to drive anyone mad, but it's worse than that. Driven mad by your own flesh – the stink of humanity. You hate your own existence, and that makes them more deadly than ever.'

Davies seems to be suggesting here that religious fanaticism is fuelled by self-loathing. There may be some truth here. Although the Christian faith at least is clear about the mess in the human heart, it also emphasises God's grace – his undeserved love and kindness to us. But when the negative side is emphasised to the detriment of the positive, it can give rise to a malign drive to make everybody and everything conform to certain standards.

All Welcome

The point of all these intolerant enemies is that they are so opposite to the Doctor. *Doctor Who* is often said to be fundamentally promoting tolerance. As Alan McKee points out in an essay on value judgements, '*Doctor Who* includes the celebration of tolerance, peaceful coexistence and the celebration of difference.'[2] The celebration of difference encompasses different race, gender and species.

In the 2005 series, diversity of sexual orientation also became something to applaud. When the Doctor, Jack and Rose go to the crash site ('The Doctor Dances'), Rose offers to distract the attention of Algy, the officer on duty, but Jack knows him and says he should go instead saying, 'He's not your type.' Rose looks uncertain, but the Doctor says, 'Relax, he's a fifty-first-century guy. He's just a bit more flexible when it comes to dancing.' 'How flexible?' Rose asks. 'By his time, you lot are spread out around the galaxy,' replies the Doctor. Rose presses him to explain. He says, 'So many species, so little time.' 'What?' exclaims Rose. 'That's what we do when we get out there? That's our mission, we seek new life and – ' 'Dance,' concludes the Doctor euphemistically.

The call for a more tolerant attitude is nothing new to *Doctor Who*. Matt Jones draws a parallel between the state on Terra Alpha trying to stamp out happiness ('The Happiness Patrol', 1988) and the opposition of Margaret Thatcher's Government to homosexuality. He writes:

> 'The Happiness Patrol' is a celebration of difference. A critique of the idea that one way of living is inherently or naturally better than any other. It outlines the horrors that occur when one group in a society rams their vision of social life down the throats of all the others. . . . you may disagree with what I've written and that's good. In fact, it's brilliant. Because if 'The Happiness Patrol' teaches us anything, it is the danger of there only being one view, one voice that shouts down all others.[3]

The message of celebrating difference and diversity is present in many of the Doctor's adventures. A good example is 'Kinda' (1982), written by Christopher Bailey. 'Kinda' was based on Ursula Le Guin's 1972 novel, *The Word for World is Forest*, and included some Buddhist ideas promoting the ideals of cooperation, communication and harmony with nature. The same themes are reinforced even by some very minor incidents through the years, as in 'Remembrance of the Daleks' when Ace is in a 1963 London boarding house run by a kindly, welcoming woman, and finds a sign in the window reading, 'No coloureds'. Ace is clearly appalled, and rightly so. Script editor Andrew Cartmel recalls being so proud of this scene, that when BBC Head of Drama Mark Shivas was distracted by a phone call, thus missing it in his official viewing of the finished programme, Cartmel insisted on his boss rewinding the tape and watching the scene:

> John [Nathan-Turner, *Doctor Who*'s producer at the time] looked at me with a combination of astonishment and amusement. But Mark Shivas indulged me. He rewound the tape. He watched the scene. He looked at me.
>
> All he said was, 'You should have had her tear up the sign'.
>
> Maybe he was right.[4]

Sylvester McCoy recalls John Nathan-Turner's account of interviewing Cartmel for the script editor's job. When asked what one thing he would want to achieve with *Doctor Who*, Cartmel apparently replied that he would want to 'overthrow the government'. Nathan-Turner decided to hire him on the spot, but replied that, 'the most he could do on a show like *Doctor Who* was get a message across about how black people and white people and green people and purple people were all equal'.[5]

When the Doctor wants to be so inclusive of an extraordinary array of species from around the galaxy, how could we possibly entertain racism here on Earth? The beginning of 'Remembrance of the Daleks' shows a shot of Earth from space with the sound of broadcasts playing. The first, in English, is a snippet from a speech of John F. Kennedy: 'Our most basic common link is that we all inhabit this small planet. We all breathe the same air. We all cherish our children's future.'[6] The implications are clear. What unites us as human beings is far more important than our differences. Diversity is something to be welcomed and celebrated, not despised. Tom Baker's Doctor waxes lyrical in 'The Ark In Space' (1975) when he sees the cryogenically preserved survivors of humanity: 'It's an amazing sight isn't it? The entire human race in one room. All colours, all creeds – all differences finally forgotten.'

It is clear that the Doctor sees intolerance as an evil attitude which results in all kinds of evil actions towards others. And, since he sees intolerance – and the closed minds which spawn it – as a root of all kinds of evil, his greatest mission is to open people's minds.

A Mission to Open Minds

The reason that the Doctor overcomes his dismissive attitude towards Rose is that she quickly demonstrates that she has an open mind. When he begins to explain her experiences with the menacing mannequins, he says, 'It's not a price war. They want to overthrow the human race and destroy you. Do you believe me?' When she replies, 'No,' the Doctor remarks, 'But you're still listening.' She is sceptical, but still open to being convinced. Although Rose falters from time to time, generally speaking she is remarkably open to what she encounters. It marks her out from many other human beings that the Doctor meets.

Although Dickens is struggling with the extraordinary new things he is encountering in Cardiff, he does also begin a determined effort to consider the possibility of being mistaken. 'Can it be,' he asks, 'that I have the world entirely wrong?' That's the right kind of question for the Doctor, who gently says to him, 'Not wrong. There's just more to learn.' By the time the danger has been averted, Dickens is on a high – not just because of the excitement, but because his whole outlook on life has been broadened. He quotes Shakespeare to the Doctor and Rose: '"There are more things in heaven and earth than are dreamt of in your philosophy." Even for you, Doctor.' Then as they part, he says, 'This morning I thought I knew everything in the world. Now I know I've just started.' That kind of sentiment is music to the Doctor's ears.

Curiously, given Adam's intelligence and his experience of alien artefacts (which admittedly, he doesn't always understand), he finds it difficult to be open-minded when he arrives on Satellite Five with Rose and the Doctor ('The Long Game'). He seems to be open to things which are new and alien as long as they remain theoretical or remote, but finds the messy business of engaging personally with them to be more challenging. When he does respond to the Doctor's instructions to throw himself into the experience, his goal is not discovery, but making a fortune from stolen technological secrets. While he is hardly being intolerant, his self-interest still falls considerably short of the Doctor's ideals.

A Better Future

As the Doctor helps people to become more receptive, so they become more able to fulfil their potential. MP

Harriet Jones is able to quickly take on board both the situation in 10 Downing Street ('World War Three') and the Doctor's approach to dealing with it. Her open mind enables her to rise to the challenges of the post-Slitheen situation and she is to become one of Britain's greatest Prime Ministers. This is the quality which, in *Doctor Who*, characterises human beings at their best. This is what has enabled them to spread through the stars.

An earlier example of the Doctor attempting to broaden people's minds is in the 'Curse of Peladon' (1972). When the Doctor first arrives, Peladon is a feudal, unenlightened society which is ruled over by a king and a high priest. The Doctor encourages the king to join the Galactic Federation in order to easily market the planet's chief raw material, tricilicate – a rare mineral previously mined only on Mars. This brings much more wealth and a new social order to the planet. But when the Doctor returns a few years later (in 'The Monster of Peladon', 1974), the king has died and his daughter has come to power – but as a puppet ruler in a still patriarchal society. The real power lies with Chancellor Ortron who remains committed to the 'ancient ways' of idol worship. He and his fellow nobles are retaining the new wealth for themselves, and the working class miners are on the point of rebelling. An external threat comes from a greedy human mining engineer and a force of Martian Ice Warriors. The Doctor urges them to move quickly towards democracy in order to deal with the internal problems – the way ahead, as far as the Doctor is concerned, is to become a society more like the progressive model of western Europe in the mid-1970s. And his companion Sarah-Jane Smith doesn't see why the young queen should be subservient to her chancellor or anyone else. She explains to the queen:

Women's liberation, your Majesty. On Earth it means
women don't let men push us around. . . . There's nothing
'only' about being a girl, your Majesty. Never mind why
they made you a queen, the fact is you *are* the Queen, so
just you jolly well let them know it.

There is an interesting tension here, at least from our
early twenty-first-century perspective. On the one
hand, the Doctor wants to liberate this society from its
subjugation to tradition, superstition and feudalism. He
and Sarah-Jane see it as their duty to bring these poor
benighted people out of their Dark Ages into a new
world of wealth, equality, democracy and co-operation
with other species. On the other hand, we could ask,
who does the Doctor think he is to interfere with
this traditional, uncomplicated society? Principles of
postmodern tolerance might argue that he should leave
well alone rather than impose his modernist, capitalist,
cultural imperialism on people who have every right to
live as they choose. The postmodern argument outlined
above coincides with the view of the Time Lords and
their strict policy of non-intervention. The Doctor's
readiness to do whatever is necessary to protect the
weak and ignorant against the dominating and strong
is at odds with this, and gets him into trouble with his
people. Perhaps the fact that we feel he is right to do
so suggests that we all know that there are limits to
tolerance: there really is injustice and evil which must
be addressed and to stand by doing nothing makes us
as culpable as the perpetrators of the evil.

A Line in the Sand

Tolerant he may be, but the Doctor is not a complete
relativist, believing that morality is simply a choice for

each individual to make. He believes in values – in good and evil. He may rebuke Rose when she objects to using Gwyneth to help the Gelth occupy dead bodies, saying, 'It is different, yeah, it's a different morality. Get used to it or go home' ('The Unquiet Dead'). But he also believes that there is a line which must not be crossed, that evil beings must be stopped. When he understands the Gelth's true intentions, he knows he must stop them – even if it means sacrificing Gwyneth. In 'Rose', the Doctor tries to persuade the Nestene Consciousness to quietly go, leaving the Earth in peace, but the monster's refusal to do so leads to its destruction. The Doctor takes some anti-plastic as 'insurance' when he goes to negotiate with the Consciousness. He genuinely does not want to destroy it, but he is prepared to do so because he will not countenance the Autons waging war on humanity. Similarly, the Slitheen must be stopped at all costs – even if the Doctor has to risk both his own life and Rose's in order to do so ('World War Three'). And again, when he runs into Margaret Slitheen a second time, the Doctor feels compelled to stop her. Script editor Helen Raynor says, 'Margaret Slitheen is essentially a hugely evil creature and it's clear he can't let her potter about Cardiff because she'll kill us all.'[7]

The Doctor is also all too aware that his greatest enemies, the Daleks, are irredeemably evil. Their intense xenophobia and their desire to overthrow and enslave or destroy the residents of other planets is not something he will tolerate. While the Doctor is at heart a tolerant, peace-loving resolver of other people's problems, there are limits. He wants to include other species in all their diversity. But how can such unmitigated evil be tolerated with a resigned shrug of the shoulders? How can such hateful beings be included in any fellowship of peaceable beings? They cannot. The Doctor exults in the destruction, as he thinks, of the Dalek race when he comes face to face with the last survivor ('Dalek'). Later, when the Dalek has escaped, the Doctor finds a weapon capable of annihilating it – but Rose stands in his way. 'That thing killed hundreds of people,' says the Doctor. 'I've got to do this. I've got to end it. The Daleks destroyed my home, my people; I've got nothing left.' We see here something of the Doctor's mixed motivations in wanting to destroy the last of the Daleks. It is not just because of the deeply evil nature of the thing, and the certainty of enormous loss of human life if it was to escape. There is also a sprinkling of vengeance in the mix. Eccleston comments:

> In 'Dalek' they expose a Doctor we haven't seen before. He becomes unreasonable and he goes mad – because he's frightened. Of all the aliens he's met, he knows their power. They are the ancient enemy of the Time Lords.[8]

At this point Rose is able to see what the Doctor can't – that maybe even a Dalek can find some redemption. And that the Doctor can also be intolerant, closed-minded and ruthless, displaying the very qualities he despises in others. She says, 'It couldn't kill van Statten; it couldn't kill me. It's changing. What about you, Doctor? What the hell are you changing into?'

The Doctor's encounter with Margaret Slitheen is interesting because of the discussion they have about the ethics of the Doctor's lifestyle. Russell T. Davies says:

> The whole point of ['Boom Town'] is to get to those scenes in the restaurant where the Doctor sits down with an enemy who he's defeated. And they get to talk to each

other and they explore the consequences of the Doctor's actions. The real story in this is who the Doctor is, and what gives him the right to live this lifestyle, and what happens afterwards. And inevitably you have to look at this and say, part of saving the world, part of that, probably involves a good few deaths. I like the Doctor's ruthlessness. I, personally, have given him a fair old streak of that just because I think it's more interesting. We're dealing with a Time Lord now who's sort of war damaged. I've always been fascinated by the fact that the Doctor is a man who always leaves.[9]

Margaret does her best to emotionally manipulate her captors, saying, 'Since you're taking me to my death, that makes you my executioners – each and every one of you.' When Mickey tells her she deserves it, she retorts, 'You're very quick to say so. You're very quick to soak your hands in my blood. Which makes you better than me how, exactly?' The Doctor points out that he does not make the law. 'But you deliver it,' says Margaret. Yes, he does. He is prepared to take her back to face death on Raxacoricofallapatorius because she is an evil creature who would happily slaughter the entire human race. She cannot be allowed to go free. Margaret tries to persuade the Doctor that she is becoming a changed character. He is not impressed:

> You let one of them go, but that's nothing new. Every now and then a little victim spared because she smiled, because he's got freckles, because they begged. And that's how you live with yourself, that's how you slaughter millions because once in a while, on a whim, if the wind's in the right direction, you happen to be kind.

Margaret turns the tables on the Doctor, suggesting that he is like her:

Only a killer would know that. Is that right? From what
I've seen, your funny little happy-go-lucky life leaves
devastation in its wake. Always moving on because you
dare not go back. Playing with so many people's lives
you might as well be a god. And you're right, Doctor,
you're absolutely right. Sometimes you let one go.

This strikes a nerve with the Doctor. He does sometimes
leave devastation in his wake; he does materialise in
a crisis, arrogantly impose his solutions on a situation
he doesn't always fully understand, and dematerialise
again without ever having to face the consequences of
his actions. He is deeply flawed. But the difference is
that he has an understanding of good and evil, and
he resolutely stands for the good against the evil.
That means he cannot always be tolerant and he must
interfere. He must attempt to do what is right and not
judge the value of every action only by its consequences,
because there are fundamental moral principles at
stake. His high-handed rashness may cause problems
at times, but that doesn't mean the overall direction of
his life is wrong.

Tolerance and Redemption

At times the Doctor's foes are offered some kind of
redemption, or at least a negotiated settlement. The
TARDIS intervenes to give Margaret Slitheen the
opportunity we all crave at times – the possibility of a
fresh start. 'The idea that you get another chance and
go back to the beginning and do it all again in the right
way is such a beautiful and seductive idea and such a
sad one as well.'[10]

'She can start again, live her life from scratch. If we take her home, give her to a different family, tell them to bring her up properly, she might be alright,' the Doctor tells Rose and Jack who replies, 'Or she might be worse.' 'That's her choice,' insists the Doctor.

We commented above on the possibility of religion going bad when only the negative side of human nature is emphasised. But when the positive side is included too – the grace of God at work in our world – it becomes something transforming. The Christian conviction in God's kindness, love and mercy to even rebellious human beings like ourselves should so move us that we, too, exemplify kindness, love and mercy. Tolerance and inclusion are at the heart of the Christian faith even more than they are at the heart of *Doctor Who*. God's concern for all people, for 'the prisoners, the refugees, the dispossessed' goes right through the Bible. But alongside it, as in *Doctor Who*, there is a clear sense that there is real good and real evil, and that lines must be drawn in the sand. If the Doctor will do whatever is necessary to defeat forces of evil, how much more will God? At the very heart of the Christian faith is the self-sacrifice of God's Son in order to both defeat evil and redeem rebellious human beings – an action which is paralleled by the Doctor's own willingness to lose his life to save others.

Like Jesus, the Doctor is intolerant of things that do not deserve to be tolerated – evil, oppression, injustice – but his opposition to these things is not a high-handed, arrogant intolerance. Such opposition is not cheap, and it sometimes demands the ultimate price of death. The Doctor can be defended from charges of cultural imperialism because he is not acting for his own benefit, but for others. More than this, he himself bears the cost of his interventions. He may tell the

Emperor Dalek that 'if there's one thing I can do, it's talk', but that is by no means the only thing that he does. He also walks the walk.

Notes

[1] Clayton Hickman, *Doctor Who Confidential: The Daleks* (BBC3, first broadcast 30 April 2005).

[2] Alan McKee, 'Which is the best *Doctor Who* story? A case study in value judgements outside the academy', *Intensities: The Journal of Cult Media*, Issue 1, Spring/Summer 2001 – www.cult-media.com/issue1/Amckee.htm.

[3] Matt Jones, 'Tory Alpha: In search of a Queer nation' in Paul Cornell (ed) *License Denied: Rumblings from the Doctor Who Underground* (Virgin, 1997), p. 56.

[4] Andrew Cartmel, *Script Doctor: The Inside Story of Doctor Who, 1986–89* (Reynolds and Hearn, 2005), p. 111.

[5] Sylvester McCoy in the foreword to Andrew Cartmel, *Script Doctor: The Inside Story of Doctor Who, 1986–89*, p. 7.

[6] Above ground nuclear testing speech by John F. Kennedy, Washington D.C., 10 June 1963. Kennedy continued, 'And we're all mortal.'

[7] Helen Raynor, *Doctor Who Confidential: Unsung Heroes and Violent Deaths*, (BBC3, first broadcast 4 June 2005).

[8] Christopher Eccleston, *Doctor Who Confidential: The Daleks*.

[9] Russell T. Davies, *Doctor Who Confidential: Unsung Heroes and Violent Deaths*.

[10] Helen Raynor, *Doctor Who Confidential: Unsung Heroes and Violent Deaths*.

9. The Empty Battlefield

Guests are reminded that Platform One forbids the use of weapons, teleportation and religion.
Platform One announcement in 'The End of the World'

It didn't take long for the 2005 series of *Doctor Who* to mention religion. The enigmatic announcement from Platform One gives rise to a number of questions. Is religion forbidden because it has been relegated to the private sphere as a matter of relatively harmless superstition, like a hobby? Is it forbidden because it is as potentially dangerous as weapons? We are left to speculate, but both attitudes towards religion have always found a place in *Doctor Who*. When Margaret Slitheen, impressed by the TARDIS' technology, likens the Doctor to a god, he replies, 'Don't worship me. I'd make a very bad god – you wouldn't get a day off for starters.' The Doctor's reply is funny and flippantly dismissive, but it also disguises the subtle assumption in Margaret's initial remark – her assessment of the Doctor's claim to deity is based solely on his superior *technology*, not on any inherent powers of his own. Again and again in *Doctor Who* (as we shall see) the supernatural is explained – or explained away – in scientific terms. This reflects the view characterised by Richard Dawkins:[1]

As time goes by and our civilization grows up more, the model of the universe that we share will become progressively less superstitious, less small-minded, less parochial. It will lose its remaining ghosts, hobgoblins and spirits, it will be a realistic model, correctly regulated and updated by incoming information from the real world.[2]

But how can Dawkins know this assertion is true before all the evidence is in? The fact is, Dawkins assumes his conclusion is true and then promises it will be justified by the evidence at some unspecified point in the future. The idea that science and religion are implacable enemies, with science slowly but surely rolling up the map of religion and consigning religious belief to the dustbin of history, is often presented as incontestable fact. But when we look closely at the arguments used by Dawkins and other champions of this view, we can see that their assumptions lack any scientific basis. In fact, the conflict is not between religion and science, but rather between religion and the philosophy of naturalism, which denies the existence of anything supernatural. As naturalist John Searle insightfully observes:

Acceptance of the current [naturalistic] views [in philosophy of mind] is motivated not so much by an independent conviction of their truth as by a terror of what are apparently the only alternatives. That is, the choice we are tacitly presented with is between a 'scientific' approach, as represented by one or another of the current versions of 'materialism', and an 'unscientific' approach, as represented by [the] traditional religious conception of the mind.[3]

However, modern science, which was given birth by the philosophical culture of Judeo-Christian religion, cannot be made synonymous with a naturalistic worldview in this way.[4]

Enduring Faith

Much science fiction proceeds as if, as on Platform One, somebody had banned religion. *Doctor Who*, by contrast, has always recognised the existence and importance of religion, even if it has generally been hostile towards it. Religious belief plays a comparatively small part in the 2005 series of *Doctor Who* (at least, it does until the arrival of the religious zealot Daleks in 'Parting of the Ways'). In previous eras of the show matters of faith were more prominent. For example, the recorded message from the First Minister of Earth to the sleeping colonists in 'The Ark In Space' (1975), awaiting the opportunity to repopulate the planet, is very much couched in the language of faith:

> You have been entrusted with a *sacred* duty to see that human culture, human knowledge, human love and *faith* shall never perish from the Universe. Guard what we have given you with all your strength. [Our italics]

While there is no direct mention of religion in the episode, how can any duty be sacred in a universe with no supernatural forces? Why is faith included in the list of human traits that are to be preserved at all costs if science has succeeded in exposing faith as another word for ignorance? The classic series of *Doctor Who* may have belittled religious faith as 'superstitious mumbo-jumbo', but it also found it impossible to fully break away from many of the assumptions of faith.

By contrast, there are few such moments in the 2005 version of *Doctor Who*. The most notable exception, apart from the fundamentalist Daleks, is Gwyneth's simple faith in 'The Unquiet Dead'. Gwyneth comes across as a very sympathetic character, wise enough to realise that Rose thinks she is stupid, and to make some astute observations about twenty-first-century life. Significantly, Gwyneth is not mocked by the Doctor for believing in an afterlife – indeed, he uses her sincere belief (which he clearly does not share himself) to convince her not to allow the Gelth through the rift. He tells her that 'if your mother and father could look down and see this, they'd tell you the same, they'd give you the strength. Now send them back!' The Doctor is willing to tap into Gwyneth's belief, but stops short of endorsing it himself. He does tell her that the Gelth aren't, as she has always thought, angels. They are disembodied aliens. Once again, science explains away the apparently supernatural.

Soul Searching

'I too used to believe in magic, but the Doctor has taught me about science. It is better to believe in science.'
                    (Leela in 'Horror of Fang Rock', 1977)

Explaining something that is apparently supernatural in scientific terms has been a staple of science fiction at least as far back as the BBC's *Quatermass and the Pit* (1967) (which reveals that Martians are the origin of human belief in devils). *Doctor Who* often reinterprets mysterious phenomena in naturalistic terms. It takes some idea that has lurked in our minds or culture for centuries and, by shining the pure, clear light of scientific reasoning onto it, exposes the scientific realities that lie beneath the spooky things we believe:

> Oriental myth cloaks a futuristic evil in 'The Talons of Weng Chiang' (1977). Egyptian myth is the source of alien evil in 'The Pyramids of Mars' (1975), and devil worship is again related to alien life in 'Image of the Fendahl' (1977). In each case, it is either future beings or alien life forms and alien technology that are revealed to be the source of mankind's superstitions and myth. In *Doctor Who*'s long history, many fans have called this a 'homage' to *Quatermass*, but it is actually out-and-out translation of Kneale's original *Quatermass and the Pit* story into Whovian terms.[5]

Constant repetition of this plot device begins to turn science fiction into 'scientism fiction', which is all about finding a physical, natural explanation for everything, including things that have so far been understood in supernatural ways. According to Simon Pegg's commentary on BBC3's *Doctor Who Confidential*: 'The Doctor has always been known for his magic touch; but behind every trick, there must be a scientific explanation.'[6] Why *must* there be a scientific explanation, unless one is assuming the truth of a naturalistic worldview? Explanations should be rational, but being rational does not necessarily mean being scientific. Arthur Chappell writes:

> *Doctor Who* tends on the whole to set science and understanding of evolution above religious belief and supernaturalism. There are undoubtedly stories in which some degree of occultism is recognised; Lady Peinforte's time travelling skills in *Silver Nemesis* (1988) are simply described as the use of 'black magic' by the Doctor, but then, he might just be using such a description of alchemy

to save himself the tedium of a longer, more detailed explanation. After all, much that we once only believed possible has now been made fully comprehensible by science . . . The implications for religion, of our knowledge of the material world growing stronger, are not the subject for optimism.[7]

Growing scientific knowledge of the material world may confirm the prejudices of some who begin with the assumption that the material world is the only world, but it is in fact the subject for optimism among a growing number of scientists and philosophers. As Michael J. Wilkins and J.P. Moreland observe:

A significant and growing number of scientists, historians of science, and philosophers of science see more scientific evidence now for a personal creator and designer than was available fifty years ago. In the light of this evidence, it is false and naive to claim that modern science has made belief in the supernatural unreasonable.[8]

In his book *Soul Searching* theoretical psychologist Nicholas Humphrey asserts that 'Few adults in the modern world can actually be unaware that there are now physicalist explanations for most if not all natural phenomena, not excluding the workings of the human mind.'[9] In point of fact, while science has given us some understanding of the human brain, it has totally failed to deliver a physicalist explanation for the workings of the human mind. Naturalist Jerry Fodor admits, 'Nobody has the slightest idea how anything material could be conscious.'[10] Fellow naturalist Ned Block concedes:

We have no conception of our physical or functional nature that allows us to understand how it could explain our subjective experience ... in the case of consciousness we have nothing – zilch – worthy of being called a research programme, nor are there any substantive proposals about how to go about starting one ... Researchers are stumped.[11]

In a public discussion between naturalists Richard Dawkins and Steven Pinker (one of the foremost contemporary writers on the brain), Dawkins said:

Neither Steven Pinker nor I can explain human subjective consciousness ... In *How the Mind Works* Steven elegantly sets out the problem of subjective consciousness, and asks where it comes from and what's the explanation. Then he's honest enough to say, 'Beats the heck out of me.' That is an honest thing to say, and I echo it. We don't know. We don't understand it.[12]

Without denying that many things do have physical explanations, we can note that to make the leap to stating that everything has a physical explanation involves a very big assumption. Indeed, this is a philosophical assumption, and one in tension with the continued failure to provide a physicalist explanation of the human mind. As philosopher of mind and naturalist John Heil admits, 'In recent years, dissatisfaction with materialist assumptions has led to a revival of interest in forms of dualism.'[13] The problem isn't simply that we haven't managed to explain the mind in physical terms yet, but that we have good reason to think that this could never be done.[14]

Scientism Friction

The urge to explain everything in purely physical terms, to have materialistic explanations swallow up everything supernatural, comes not from science itself, but from over-emphasising the abilities and value of science. This scientistic view believes that *only* scientific knowledge, conceived of as material explanations about material realities, is reliable and trustworthy. Nicholas Humphrey promotes scientism when he says that all human beings are by nature 'minor natural scientists' even though 'they do of course also sometimes employ other less reliable (and less effective) ways to gaining knowledge.'[15] Richard Dawkins is stronger when he says:

> Next time somebody tells you something that sounds important, think to yourself: 'Is this the kind of thing that people probably know because of evidence? Or is it the kind of thing that people only believe because of tradition, authority or revelation?' And next time somebody tells you that something is true, why not say to them: 'What kind of evidence is there for that?' And if they can't give you a good answer, I hope you'll think very carefully before you believe a word they say.[16]

So, evidence is good – it's scientific – whereas tradition, authority and revelation aren't. The implication seems to be that you can't believe anything which the latter three tell you unless there is also scientific evidence. Religious people are automatically to be considered as irrational and childish, because they believe extraordinary things on the basis of inadequate evidence. Richard Dawkins says that 'When religious people just have a feeling inside themselves that something must be true, even though there is no evidence that it is true, they call their feeling "revelation".'[17] On this definition of revelation, Dawkins' belief that the only way to know things is through evidence may itself count as a revelation – after all, he can't have any evidence for it. Hence, according to Dawkins' own advice, it is a bad reason for believing anything.

It is true that for Christian theology, 'revelation' can mean a private revelation – an individual religious experience in which God is taken to be imparting knowledge. But it can also mean a public revelation, such as a miracle. In either case, revelation can involve publicly knowable and testable evidence (such as the wealth of historical evidence for Jesus' resurrection).[18]

Bland Faith

Doctor Who, like many naturalists, sees faith as a matter of subjective personal opinion wholly unconnected to reason or evidence. In 'The Curse of Fenric' (1989) the vampire-like haemovores are repelled by people's faith; but it is the faith itself that counts and not the *truth* of the faith. They are kept at bay by Captain Sorin's faith in the Communist revolution just as much as by the Rev. Wainwright's (failing) faith in God or Ace's faith in the Doctor. Faith is portrayed, as the Doctor himself says, as nothing more than 'confidence'.

In 'The Daemons' (1971) (a story inspired by *Quatermass and the Pit*), Jon Pertwee's Doctor combats an animated gargoyle by pointing at it with a trowel and exclaiming, 'Klokleda partha mennin klatch!' When companion Jo asks the Doctor why this worked, he explains that iron is 'an old magical defence'. Jo objects that the Doctor doesn't believe in magic. 'I don't', he replies, 'But he did ... luckily!' And the 'spell' that he recited was 'the first line of an old Venusian lullaby.' Yet again, something with supernatural associations is shown working merely on the basis of belief rather than truth. Similarly, in 'Father's Day' the church becomes a place of refuge from the Reapers, not because it is a holy place, but simply because it is old. That a belief stands the test of time, or even that it works to some extent, is no guarantee of its truth.[19]

Atheist Julian Baggini defines belief in the supernatural as 'belief in what there is a lack of strong evidence to believe in. Indeed, sometimes it is belief in something that is contrary to the available evidence ... religious belief is a faith position because it goes beyond what there is evidence or argument for.'[20] It is easy to take statements like this at face value, but anyone familiar with the traditions of Christian theology, philosophy and apologetics would recognise the flaw in the statement. Far from being competitors to one another, faith and reason happily coexist in Christianity, as Wilkins and Moreland point out:

> New Testament religion tells us to love God with the mind (Matthew 22:37), to have an answer in the form of good reasons for why we believe what we believe (1 Peter 3:15), and to accept that God wishes to reason together with his creatures (Isaiah 1:18), and to believe that human reason, though fallen [damaged], is still part of the image of God within us (Acts 17:27–28) and continues to be a gift we are to cultivate and exercise. Thus, the modern view of faith as something unrelated or even hostile to reason is a departure from traditional Christianity and not a genuine expression of it.[21]

Baggini astonishingly represents the story of doubting Thomas,[22] who refused to accept the eye-witness testimony of ten friends for the reality of Jesus' resurrection (but subsequently accepted the resurrection as true once he himself had met with the risen Jesus[23]), as endorsing 'the principle that it is good to believe what you have no evidence to believe.'[24] But in fact

Jesus commends people who believe *without having to see for themselves*, not those who believe *without evidence*. There are other types of evidence than what we see for ourselves. Thomas had already been presented with testimony from witnesses to Jesus' post-resurrection appearance, people who he knew and trusted. He had seen the change of heart that had come over the other disciples who, like him, had been in despair at the death of their leader. When Jesus chose to appear before Thomas, it provided the most compelling evidence that Thomas could hope for, but without this, he was hardly being asked to believe on no basis at all. As Roger Steer writes:

> Faith is not a blind leap in the dark, but personal trust based on rational argument and the weighing of evidence ... Jesus had respect for Thomas' demand for evidence. There was no expectation that the sceptical disciple should exercise blind trust in the absence of evidence ... of course, generations of people since then have been invited to exercise faith without the privilege of sight granted to Thomas, but the point is that through the centuries followers of Christ have never been required to take a step – or make a leap – which is blind or irrational.[23]

Scientism in *Doctor Who*

The problem with scientism is that it over-values what science can do. It sounds scientific to talk in these terms about evidence, but it isn't. Scientism is a misuse of science and it is not scientific. The reason is, quite simply, that you cannot prove it scientifically. What scientific evidence is there that you need scientific evidence before you believe something? How could you have any such evidence without needing evidence for the reality of that evidence, and so on to infinity?

How do you scientifically prove that *only* scientific knowledge is valid? Can you even prove that you must be able to prove things before you believe them?

The whole of science is, in fact, based on philosophical assumptions which are inherently non-scientific. For example, we assume that the laws of nature will carry on being the same in all places at all times – an experiment done in Cardiff in 1869 will give the same result when repeated during the fourth great and bountiful human empire two hundred millennia from now. That may well be the case, but it is an empirically unprovable assumption rather than a provable scientific fact.[26] Christians believe that the universe is both created and sustained by God, a view which provides a reasonable basis for making such an assumption – the laws of nature are consistent because God made them that way.

Scientism often pops up in *Doctor Who* as an assumption in the background rather than as something argued for head on. In 'The Unquiet Dead', the premises of Mr Sneed the undertaker are the scene of some very strange goings-on. The dead are getting up out of their coffins and going walkabout. When old Mrs. Peace does the same and keeps her appointment to hear the great Charles Dickens, she causes a stampede when a spectral emanation comes out of her and whirls around the theatre moaning in time-honoured ghostly fashion. The scene has strong echoes of the ectoplasm that Victorian spiritualists fraudulently claimed they saw in their séances. Later, in Mr Sneed's premises, Dickens is dismayed to hear the Doctor insisting on the reality of these spirits. He complains:

> But I've always railed against the fantasist. Oh, I've loved an illusion as much as the next man – revelled in

them. But that's exactly what they were: illusions. The real world is something else. I dedicated my life to that – injustices, the great social causes. Now you tell me that the real world is a realm of spectres and jack-o-lanterns. In which case, have I wasted my brief span here, Doctor? Has it all been for nothing?

And a little later, he refuses to take part in the séance saying:

This is precisely the sort of cheap mummery I strive to unmask. Séances? Nothing but luminous tambourines and a squeezebox concealed between the knees.

The picture we get of *Doctor Who*'s Dickens is of a man with a great and highly rational mind who refuses to believe in magic or mystery. He values science rather than superstition, but he now finds himself faced with inexplicable realities. The turning point comes when he finally understands events in the same way as the Doctor: these are not ghosts but real, physical – although gaseous – beings from another part of the universe (somewhat further than Brecon, which is about as far as Mr Sneed can imagine).

Likewise, Gwyneth's ability to communicate with 'her angels' and her second sight are explained as due to the fact that she has lived her life over a rift in space and time. It has enabled her to perceive things which all our normal expectations would say are impossible. But she has just been caught up in the fabric of space and time in an unusual way: 'Living on the rift, she's become part of it,' says the Doctor. The psychic phenomena displayed by Gwyneth have a physical (scientific) basis, albeit one which is still beyond human understanding. In 'Image of the Fendahl'

(1977) the Doctor similarly explains the precognitive abilities of Ma Tyler as the result of a childhood spent near a time fissure.

Through the repetition of such incidents, *Doctor Who* builds up the expectation that all apparently supernatural phenomena must have a naturalistic, 'scientific' explanation. The Doctor's assertion, made in 'The Horror of Fang Rock' (1977), that 'there's nothing supernatural going on around here', becomes an unquestionable assumption set in stone. However, to approach real life claims about the supernatural (for example, claims about miracles, angelic encounters, demon possession, or religious experiences of God[27]) with this expectation in hand risks automatically dismissing genuine evidence to the contrary. Although face-saving interpretations like Arthur Chappell's comments about Lady Peinforte (quoted above) are always a possibility, on the face of things even *Doctor Who* contains occasional examples of apparently genuine supernatural, occult or magical powers. Examples include not only Lady Peinforte, but also the immaterial Great Intelligence in 'The Abominable Snowmen' (1967), Shurr the Seeker in 'The Ribos Operation' (1978), and the sorceress Morgaine in 'Battlefield' (1989).

This observation cuts across the stereotype (illustrated by the blasphemy-condemning Daleks in 'Parting of the Ways') that religion narrows one's intellectual horizons while science broadens them. If science is replaced by scientism, quite the reverse can be true. After all, one needn't make the opposite assumption (i.e. that all supernatural claims are genuine) to keep an open mind on the subject. Following Occam's razor (always choose the simplest adequate explanation), one can give pride of place to naturalistic explanations when they suffice, whilst remaining open to the possibility that a supernatural explanation might turn out to be the best explanation of the facts on any given occasion.

In 'The Face of Evil' (1977), the Doctor makes the following statement:

> The very powerful and the very stupid have one thing in common: they don't alter their views to fit the facts, they alter the facts to fit their views.

Although the Doctor is describing the leaders of Leela's tribe, the Servateem, and in particular their adherence to a supernatural religion which is subsequently revealed to be (surprise, surprise) based on ignorance of scientific and historical fact, his statement can equally cut in the opposite direction. When the possibility of anything supernatural is dismissed out of hand because we 'know' that science is steadily disproving 'that kind of thing', we are in danger of distorting the evidence to fit our pre-ordained verdict.

Having an open mind and thinking outside of the box are character traits that *Doctor Who* enthusiastically endorses. In 'Mark of the Rani' (1985) the sixth Doctor rails against the evil Rani's soul-denying materialistic philosophy. Quoting the same Shakespearean line that Charles Dickens echoes at the end of 'The Unquiet Dead', the Doctor warns that she should 'accept there are more things in heaven and earth than are dreamt of in your barren philosophy'.

Notes

1. Dawkins, incidentally, is now married to Lalla Ward, who was the second actress to play the companion Romana in *Doctor Who* (1979–1981).

2   Richard Dawkins, *Royal Institute Christmas Lecture*, 1991, Lecture 5, 'The genesis of purpose'.

3   John Searle, *Rediscovery of the Mind* (MIT Press, 1992), p. 3–4.

4   cf. Michael Bumbulis, 'Christianity and the Birth of Science' at www.ldolphin.org/bumbulis/; James Hannam, 'Christianity and the Rise of Science' at www.bede.org. uk/sciencehistory.htm; Eric V. Snow, 'Christianity, a cause of modern science?' at www.rae.org/jaki.html; Charles Thaxton, 'Christianity and the Scientific Enterprise' at www.leaderu.com/truth/1truth17.html.

5   John Kenneth Muir, *A Critical History of Doctor Who on Television* (McFarland, 1999), p. 46.

6   *Doctor Who Confidential: Weird Science*, (BBC3, first broadcast 28 May 2005).

7   Arthur Chappell, 'The meaning of belief and religion in Dr. Who' at www.arthurchappell.clara.net/religion.in.dr. who.htm.

8   Michael J. Wilkins & J.P. Moreland, *Jesus Under Fire* (Paternoster, 1995), p. 10.

9   Nicholas Humphrey, *Soul Searching* (Chatto and Windus, 1995), p. 7.

10 Jerry Fodor, 'The Big Idea: Can There Be A Science of Mind?', *Times Literary Supplement*, 3 July 1992, p. 5.

11 Ned Block, 'Consciousness', in Samuel Guttenplan (ed.) *A Companion to Philosophy of Mind* (Blackwell, 1994), p. 211.

12 Richard Dawkins, quoted by Varghese, *The Wonder of the World*, (Tyr, 2004), p. 56.

13 John Heil, *Philosophy of Mind – a contemporary introduction* (Routledge, 1998), p. 53. Dualism is the belief that the human mind is more than a merely physical thing, and that it consists, either in whole or in part, of an immaterial, non-physical reality which is often called 'soul' or 'spirit'.

14 cf. William Hasker, *The Emergent Self* (Cornell University Press, 2001); J.P. Moreland, *Scaling the Secular City* (Baker, 1987); Victor Reppert, *C.S. Lewis's Dangerous Idea* (IVP, 2003); Richard Swinburne, *The Evolution of the Soul* (Clarendon Press, 1997); Charles Taliaferro, *Consciousness and the Mind*

of God, (Cambridge University Press, 2005).

15 Nicholas Humphrey, *Soul Searching*, p. 53.

16 Richard Dawkins, *A Devil's Chaplain*, p. 248.

17 Richard Dawkins, *A Devil's Chaplain*, p. 245.

18 For an academic study of the evidence, cf. William Lane Craig, *The Son Rises* (Wipf & Stock, 2001). For an easier read, see Josh McDowell, *The Resurrection Factor* (Thomas Nelson, 1993).

19 Richard Dawkins gave the concept of an idea that endures because of its catchiness, rather than any inherent truth, the name 'meme'. The Adherents of the Repeating Meme in 'The End of the World' derive their title from this.

20 Julian Baggini, *Atheism: A Very Short Introduction* (Oxford University Press, 2003), p. 32.

21 Michael Wilkins & J.P. Moreland, *Jesus Under Fire* (Paternoster, 1996), p. 8.

22 cf. Ralph F. Wilson, 'Learning Faith from Doubting Thomas' at www.leaderu.com/theology/doubting_thomas.html.

23 Jn. 20:24–29.

24 Julian Baggini, *Atheism: A Very Short Introduction*, p. 33.

25 Roger Steer, *Letter to an Influential Atheist* (Authentic Lifestyle/Paternoster, 2003), p. 137–138.

26 cf. Wade A. Tisthammer, 'The Nature and Philosophy of Science' at www.angelfire.com/mn2/tisthammerw/science. html#_ednref14.

27 cf. Peter S. Williams, *The Case for Angels* (Paternoster, 2003).

10. A Great Life

If you can't kill, then what are you good for, Dalek? What's the point of you?
The Doctor in 'Dalek'

The Doctor's question to the Dalek in Henry van Statten's museum is a good one, and one which can be legitimately turned back on the Doctor himself. If we were to ask what the point of the Doctor's life is, we might get one of two answers. In 'Aliens of London' he tells Rose that the reason he travels is 'to see history happening' – he is spurred by the thrill of exploration, of discovery, of satisfying his curiosity. At the same time, the Doctor recognises that it isn't enough just to wander through the cosmos like a tourist. As we have seen, our hero can't stop himself from intervening. When something is wrong he is quite prepared to put himself in the line of fire in order to put it right. More than this, he relishes the opportunity, exclaiming 'Fantastic' at the first sign of any drama that he can throw himself into.

When Rose sums up what she has learned from travelling with the Doctor, she focuses on the second of these two lines of thought, pointing out to Mickey in 'Parting of the Ways' that the Doctor has shown them a better way of living, one where 'you don't give up, you don't just let things happen. You make a stand, you say "no", you've the guts to do what's right when everyone else runs away.'

In his holographic message to Rose in 'Parting of the Ways', the Doctor's sole instruction was to 'have a great life', and it is clear that he means more than just having a fun time. The Doctor leaves Rose with the responsibility of making her life count. To paraphrase the Editor (completely out of context), he tells her not to walk through the world without leaving a footprint.

Rose's experience of travelling with the Doctor has given her a new sense of meaning and purpose for her life. She can no longer be content with the humdrum existence she knew before. Even if she had not been able to get back to the Games Station, even if she had remained stuck on Earth in her own time, we know that Rose wouldn't have simply slotted back in to the undemanding life that she had previously lived, because she now knew that life was meant to be something more than just existing.

Of course, *Doctor Who* also presents us with several other responses to the question 'what's the point of you?'

It Still Comes Down to Money

Our first sighting of Christopher Eccleston's Doctor is in the bowels of a London department store, and after that commercially-tinged entrance, the issue of money is never far from the surface for the rest of the series. *Doctor Who* has sometimes been mocked for having the Doctor save the world week after week, story after story. But in the 2005 version the vast cosmic schemes that he pits himself against often seem to be grounded in the mundane motivation of financial gain.

The reasons for this are partly because Russell T. Davies has worked hard to avoid slipping into cliché with his treatment of that melodramatic archetype, the evil genius:

> We haven't got any real evil geniuses because I don't believe they exist, actually. I think you're writing nonsense when you write someone who sits there going, 'Hahaha, I'm going to destroy the world.' It's like I don't actually believe them, and whenever we come across a character who might be in the place of an evil genius, we try to give it motivation and background and depth and good dialogue and a sense of humour as well, so they're not nonsense cardboard characters.[1]

Many of the new generation who stand in the place of evil geniuses reflect our own human tendency to obsess about money. Cassandra's sabotage of Platform One had purely financial objectives; the Slitheen are less concerned with global domination than with global marketing – selling the Earth as a radioactive fuel source; Henry van Statten sees the delights and wonders of the universe entirely in terms of how they can make him richer; and the Editor works under the Jagrafess to enslave humanity, but does so because he represents a consortium of banks. Even sometime TARDIS crewmembers Adam and Jack are criticised by the Doctor for their respective attempts to make a little money on the side. Indeed, only the Daleks and the Gelth offer us *Doctor Who* enemies with the more traditional purpose of conquest for its own sake. Time and time again we are given a warning of what can happen when the pursuit of money is given pride of place in our ambitions. It seems to suggest something fundamental to human nature. As the Doctor himself says to Cassandra, 'Five billion years and it still comes down to money.'

Cassandra, the Slitheen, van Statten and the Editor all share another characteristic: their desire for financial gain is so strong that it completely overpowers any misgivings about the consequences for other people. All three show no compunction whatsoever in killing anyone who gets in their way. For them it is clear that greed is not only good, it is the only thing worth taking seriously.

The Editor tries to defend his employment with philosophical musings, which the Doctor cuts dismissively through. The only thing he says which offers any meaningful explanation of his actions is that 'money prefers a long-term investment'. Margaret Slitheen says that she would blow up a whole planet, along with everyone on it, 'like stepping on an anthill'. Cassandra defends her actions by rhetorically asking, 'Do you think it's cheap looking like this? Flatness costs a fortune.' Although her original plan was to manufacture a hostage situation and gain huge amounts of compensation, she is just as happy to teleport off Platform One and leave the others to face certain death, secure in the knowledge that her share holdings in their rival companies will triple once news of their deaths becomes public. When the Doctor reverses her teleportation feed, she is overheard boasting about what she did to 'the little aliens' as she rematerialises.

While bullets are flying as van Statten's troops try to prevent the lone Dalek from escaping, van Statten barks orders for them to stop firing, dismissing his soldiers as 'dispensable', in contrast to his unique exhibit. He is more concerned with avoiding scratches on the Dalek's bodywork than with the lives of his fellow humans. Chillingly, after he issues his command all noise of battle promptly ceases, but only because the Dalek has wiped out the whole section of guards. Earlier, as van

Statten examines the Doctor, he is chided by the Time Lord, who compares his host unfavourably with the Dalek:

> Do you know what a Dalek is van Statten? A Dalek is honest. It does what it was born to do for the survival of its species. That creature in your dungeon is better than you.

To which van Statten replies that 'in that case, I will be true to myself and continue'. Van Statten has no interest in anybody else's life. All that matters to him is self-interest and adding to his already vast wealth. The casual way that he discards staff who have outstayed their usefulness, wiping their memories and dumping them on the roadside in 'Memphis, Minneapolis, someplace beginning with M' sums up his absolute disregard for anything beyond self-interest. Even when he offers to help the Doctor to bypass the computerised security shut-outs, he makes it clear that he is doing so only because he doesn't want to die. As for the Dalek's sense of purpose, we will return to that later.

Small Change

While Jack and Adam clearly fall a long way short of the callous disregard of others embodied by Cassandra, van Statten and company, they still find themselves being judged unfavourably by the Doctor. Adam is dismissed from the TARDIS crew after he is caught trying to turn time travel to his own financial advantage. He may claim that he 'would give anything' to get into space and travel among the stars, but when his dream finally comes true he shows that his true motives are closer to those of his old mentor, van Statten, than his new one. He may not set out to hurt anyone, but equally the only person who he seems interested in helping is himself. It is hard to feel that the Doctor has dealt harshly with him.

Similarly, the Doctor is scathing of Jack's scam in 'The Empty Child' and 'The Doctor Dances'. Jack may not have meant any harm by it, with only the gullible Time Agents intended to suffer in his scheme, but the end result was very nearly the end of human life on Earth. It takes Jack quite a while to accept any responsibility for what he has done, but once he realises the consequences of his actions, he is quick to make amends. Although our first encounter with Jack suggests a shallow rogue with an eye for the main chance, the Jack who dies (albeit temporarily) in 'Parting of the Ways' is morally unrecognisable from the version of himself who wooed Rose under the shadow of Big Ben. As with Rose, exposure to life with the Doctor has brought about a revision of his sense of values, and a new realisation that some things in life are more important than lining your pockets.

Metaltron and Meaning

The Doctor's first encounter with the solitary Dalek in van Statten's underground bunker is a classic *Doctor Who* moment. Once we realise who he is dealing with, we are left with no illusions about the goals that the monster will pursue:

> *Doctor*: Look, I'm sorry about this. I've come to help. I'm
>   the Doctor . . .'
> *Dalek*: (slowly) Doc-tor?

Doctor: (alarmed) Impossible!
Dalek: (quicker) *The* Doctor? Exterminate! Exterminate!
Exterminaaaaaaaaaaaaate!

The impact of the scene was possibly reduced by the fact that the BBC had been showing it as a trailer for the show, thus removing any suspense about who or what 'Metaltron' would turn out to be. Nevertheless, as the Doctor heard the distinctive metallic voice, he knew that he was dealing with a ruthless killing machine, one which wouldn't think twice before destroying anything that crossed its path. As it says later to Rose, 'I am armed, I will kill. It is my purpose.' Daleks have been genetically engineered for the sole purpose of establishing their own race as the supreme force in the universe. To this end, all emotions except hate have been discarded as unnecessary weaknesses. Daleks are bred to be perfect soldiers – unwavering of purpose, ruthlessly committed to the goal of absolute Dalek domination.

To Be or Not To Be

But the solitary Dalek in 'Dalek' has a problem. Two unrelated factors cause it to start questioning its purpose in life. The first factor is its isolation. For years the Dalek was stranded on Earth, drained of power and cut off from other Daleks. When it meets the Doctor it discovers that it is the last of its kind (or at least, that's what we were all meant to think for another six episodes). As the realisation that there is no-one left to provide it with orders sinks in, the Doctor taunts the Dalek: 'You're just a soldier without commands.' True to its conditioning, the Dalek responds by announcing

'I shall follow the primary order, the Dalek instinct to destroy, to conquer.' But the Doctor draws its attention to the pointlessness of that course of action – how can the Dalek seek to establish the Daleks in what they feel to be their rightful place as the supreme race in the universe, when the Dalek race has already been wiped off the face of space and time as a result of the Time War? If the Doctor is right and the Daleks have already failed, then the standing orders are pointless.

The second factor is one which the Dalek brings on itself. In order to restore power to its systems, the Dalek plays on Rose's sympathy (her human weakness, as it would undoubtedly see it). When she lays a comforting hand on the Dalek's metal casing, it extrapolates her time-traveller's DNA (more potent, it appears, than the DNA of those who haven't voyaged in the fourth dimension – when van Statten's henchmen touched the Dalek they went up in flames). This enables the Dalek to regenerate its dying cells and return to full working order. But this new lease of life comes at a cost to the Dalek, and it begins to mutate into something new, with Rose's humanity infecting the purebred Dalek nature.

Fortunately for the sake of the storyline (but unfortunately for van Statten's hapless henchmen) these two factors don't bring about an immediate change in the Dalek's attitude. The creature goes on a killing spree, laying waste to countless soldiers and technicians in the process. But finding itself alone with Rose in its sights, the Dalek is unable to exterminate her. Similarly, when it finally confronts van Statten, who had jailed and tortured it, extermination does not follow. As Rose explains to the Doctor, the Dalek has started to question itself.

For humans, self-questioning is an accepted part of normal life. For a Dalek it is a new and frightening experience. As we saw in Chapter 5, a central tenet of *Doctor Who* is that humanity is at its best when asking questions and seeking a worthwhile purpose in life. The humans who the Doctor is most dismissive of tend to be those who blindly accept the status quo, like the journalists on Satellite Five, or the employees of the Games Station. As the Dalek cries 'exterminate', its weapon fires either side of Rose, and it looks to her for an explanation of this failing: 'You have given me life. What else have you given me?' Later, as the mutation takes a firmer hold on the Dalek's consciousness, it shows a desire to experience the feel of sunlight, but also comments, 'This is not life, this is sickness. I shall not be like you.' The prospect of life as 'Dalek plus' is so horrific, that in a fit of existential angst it asks Rose to order it to die.

Beyond Doctor and Dalek

The plight of the solitary Dalek has parallels with the experience of humans in real life. For thousands of years, the vast majority of humans accepted belief in some kind of supernatural power which has made the world and everyone in it. Relatively recently, in the last couple of centuries, more people began to doubt whether such a being really exists. It was left to the nineteenth-century philosopher Friedrich Nietzsche to point out some of the consequences of such a shift in belief. Nietzsche argued that if you remove belief in God from human thought, you have to change the entire way that we make sense of the world. With no God, there can be no absolute moral values and no objective purpose, meaning or value to human existence. If there is nobody who made us, then by definition, we cannot be made for a purpose. Moreover, without God, we are forced to move beyond good and evil – with no God, there can be no right or wrong.[2]

The contemporary British philosopher Julian Baggini has described this as a public relations problem for atheism – how to get around the perception of atheists as people who 'believe that there is no God and no morality; or no God and no meaning to life.'[3] This is indeed a problem, particularly because Baggini agrees with Nietzsche that this is precisely the case. The solution Baggini offers is that 'we can choose our own purposes ... and thus be the authors of our own meaning.'[4]

Baggini argues that for us to choose our own purpose in life is preferable to having one imposed on us by a creator. He argues that a knife may well have been made for a purpose, but this purpose has no significance for the knife itself. Therefore a purpose that is imposed upon us from an outside force, rather than one that we choose for ourselves, will be less meaningful.

But there is a big difference between a human (or even a Dalek) and a piece of cutlery. Humans and Daleks are sentient, self-aware creatures; a knife is not – meaning that any purpose would be meaningless for the knife itself, as the knife has no perception of anything. It is an inanimate object.

There is another problem with the view that self-chosen subjective purpose is superior to God-given purpose. There is an important difference between having a purpose that is *meaningful* (in that it is a good purpose to have), and having a purpose that is *meaningless* (because it is not a good purpose to have). All of the characters from *Doctor Who* mentioned in this chapter have a sense of purpose. For the Doctor it is discovery and righting wrongs, for the Daleks it is universal domination, for Cassandra, van Statten and several others it is the pursuit of wealth and power. Obviously, the fact that a character has a purpose does not mean that their purpose is a good one. Van Statten chooses the callous pursuit of wealth and power as his purpose, the Doctor chooses discovery and protecting the weak. If we have to move with Nietzsche 'beyond good and evil' in a world without God, then we cannot say that one purpose is better than the other. The most we can say is that they are different.

Daleks have a clear, objective, given purpose – they are literally made to kill and to conquer. It could be argued that Margaret Slitheen had a given purpose because of the particular family environment she was born into. But in neither case can those given purposes be seen as being objectively good. In that sense, we cannot say that they have meaningful lives. The goals that Margaret and the Daleks each pursue lack the worth that we instinctively feel intelligent life should aim towards. Both Margaret and the Daleks suffer from a restricted sense of freedom of choice, and show a profound disregard for anybody else's freedom of choice – and again, this goes against our sense of what a meaningful life should be like. Similarly, when we discover in 'Bad Wolf' that the controller of the Games Station was chosen by the Daleks at the age of five for her role, we do not feel that she has got a particularly good deal. Her life has been given a clear purpose, imposed upon it by the Daleks, but it is not one which we feel is good for her or for others.

A given purpose is not necessarily a meaningful, worthwhile purpose. A purpose is only meaningful if it conforms to a clear, objective moral basis – which requires precisely the sort of objective moral framework that Nietzsche and Baggini both say is impossible to hold onto once God is removed from the equation. With no God there can be no objective right and wrong, and therefore no objective way to judge one purpose against another. Who is to say, in a world of relative values, that the Doctor is right in condemning the Daleks? Who is to say that Cassandra is not justified in leaving a trail of dead behind her on Platform One? Who is to say that the Doctor's urge to save the world is better than Margaret Slitheen's urge to destroy it?

And yet we do say precisely these things. Nobody watches *Doctor Who* and thinks, 'I hope the Daleks win this time, they deserve it.'[5] We know that the Doctor is on the side of right. Sometimes he is faced with a foe who is misguided rather than evil (for example, the nanogenes in 'The Empty Child' and 'The Doctor Dances'), and sometimes his actions have unforeseen consequences that are bad (such as the way his actions in 'The Long Game' led to the morally feeble humans a century later in 'Bad Wolf'). Nevertheless, the audience is left in no doubt that the Doctor's sense of purpose is a noble and fundamentally good one. What he represents is clearly better than what Daleks, or Slitheen, or Gelth represent. And yet, if we have discarded the basis for an objective moral framework, there can be no truth in such an assessment. Indeed, there can be no such thing as 'better than' at all. If all meaning and purpose is subjective, then it is no better to save the world than to destroy it.

The Only Thing That Matters

Few people would take seriously Jack's quip in 'Bad Wolf' that maximizing one's own pleasure is 'the only thing that matters in the end'. The way that he dies shows that even he doesn't really believe this – unless running around corridors fighting a hopeless cause against invading Daleks is his idea of having fun. The Doctor may give every indication of enjoying the thrill of dangerous situations, but there is more to his way of life than the cosmic equivalent of bungee jumping. In 'World War Three' he says, 'This is my life, Jackie. It's not fun, it's not smart, it's just standing up and making a decision because nobody else will.' The Doctor feels a compulsion to do what is right, to protect those who are unable to protect themselves. He recognises that he has knowledge and abilities that make him uniquely suited to fighting evil throughout time and space, and that is what he does.

And that is what we love the Doctor for. We love Rose and Jack because they are also willing to sacrifice their lives for a good cause, rather than being willing to sacrifice lots of other people's lives for their own self-interest. It is clear that the choices made by the main characters are better morally than those made by the villains of the various episodes. Not that the main characters are always right – Rose challenges the Doctor about his eagerness to kill in 'Dalek'; the Doctor accuses Rose of being more interested in 'the Universe doing something for you' than with discovery in 'Father's Day' – but we know that at their core, they have a sense of purpose that is basically right because it really is *good*. In 'The Long Game' the Editor asks the Doctor, 'How can you walk through the world and not leave a single footprint?' This is ironic, because the lives that the Doctor and Rose lead are the opposite of that – they are lives of meaningful purpose which make a significant difference to countless other people.

This is what the Doctor means by having 'a great life'. The question is, can any life be 'great' if God does not exist? There may be no God in *Doctor Who*, but the fact that we, the audience, regard the lives of the main characters as being worthwhile, meaningful and undeniably a good thing can only make sense if our world has a creator who provides a basis for our understanding of anything being objectively good.

Notes

[1] Russell T. Davies, *Doctor Who Confidential: The Dark Side* (BBC3, first broadcast 7 May 2005).

[2] www.age-of-the-sage.org/philosophy/friedrich_nietzsche_quotes.html.

[3] Julian Baggini, *Atheism: A Very Short Introduction* (Oxford University Press, 2003), p. 3.

[4] Julian Baggini, *Atheism: A Very Short Introduction*, p. 62.

[5] Unless the episode features Adric or Mel as companions, in which case more power to your pointy guns, you metallic fiends.

11. Monsters from Outer Space?

I know it sounds incredible, but I honestly believe the whole universe is just teeming with life.
Adam in 'Dalek'

Most *Doctor Who* monsters have a 'scientific' explanation: they are aliens. Some of them are related to humans: the Doctor tells Rose that humanity's great mission within the community of space-travellers is interbreeding as widely and actively as possible. Some, such as Cassandra, may have disapproved of such actions, but the humans of *Doctor Who*'s future generally have impeccable multi-cultural credentials. The fact that this explains the high frequency of humanoid bipedal aliens, thus saving time and money in costume and special effects for other species, is a happy side-effect of this particular addition to the mythology of the show.

Not all aliens in *Doctor Who* are part of the wider human family. From the Moxx of Balhoon to the Slitheen family from Raxacoricofallapatorius, the Universe is chock-a-block full with non-human life. That has always been the assumption of most popular science fiction, *Doctor Who* included. (It would be much duller if the opposite were assumed: the Doctor arrives on a new planet. He hangs around for a bit then leaves because there's nobody there whose schemes he can foil. It's another mini adventure.) The same assumption underlies today's scientific 'Search for Extra-Terrestrial Intelligence' (SETI).[1]

Aliens and Religious Belief

Although popular belief in aliens has died down from a peak in the late 1970s, most people still believe in the existence of ETI. According to a 1999 survey by popular science magazine *Focus*, 50.2 per cent of British people think that alien life must exist in the universe somewhere.[2] 60 per cent of Americans polled by the *National Geographic Channel* in 2005 said they believe life exists on other planets.[3] Majority belief does not necessarily mean that a thing is true, but if it were, what implications would the existence of aliens have for religious belief? A 1999 NASA report on the 'Societal Implications of Astrobiology' affirmed: 'the search for extraterrestrial life ... offers a meeting ground not only for physical, biological and social scientists, but also for ... philosophers, theologians.'[4] In other words, SETI is about trying to understand our place in the scheme of things, not merely scientifically, but metaphysically, in terms that inform our worldview. Many people expect that knowing whether we are alone in the universe, or are just a small part of a menagerie of intelligent life, must have a profound impact on not only our science, but our philosophy and religion too.

Of course, Christians have never thought that humanity is alone in the universe. God may be far beyond our control or understanding, but at the same time Christians believe that he involves himself with his creation – Emmanuel, one of the names given to Jesus, literally means 'God with us'. The options are not limited to belief in aliens or belief that we are all alone in the universe, unless you subscribe to a specifically atheist worldview. However, some Christians have believed (and do believe) that humans are the only embodied creatures in creation to be made in God's image,[5] and some atheists therefore suggest that, 'if and when one ever detects evidence of an extraterrestrial [intelligence] that evidence will be inconsistent with the existence of God, or at least organised religion.'[6] For example, philosopher Theodore Schick thinks the discovery of aliens would be catastrophic for Christianity:

> Since humanists believe that life is a natural rather than a supernatural phenomenon, they have no trouble admitting that self-conscious, intelligent beings may exist elsewhere in the universe. Such an admission is not so easy for Christians ... The Bible does not mention the existence of other planets, let alone intelligent creatures that inhabit them ... if intelligent aliens were discovered, Christian theologians would have a lot of explaining to do.[7]

However, the only assumption that would be threatened by discovering advanced alien life is the assumption that humanity is the *sole* end and pinnacle of God's creation; and the Bible simply doesn't make this assumption. While it has nothing to say about the existence of aliens from other planets, neither does it have anything to say about their non-existence – it is simply silent on the issue. It seems that the leaders of the Church of England similarly make no such link between the likelihood of intelligent alien life and the validity of their faith: according to a poll conducted by *The Sunday Times*, 40 out of 42 Bishops (95 per cent) said that life could exist on other planets. Thirty-one (74 per cent) said that alien life could be intelligent.[8]

Schick presents a false dilemma between viewing life as a product of the inherent capacities of nature (i.e. something that evolved) or as the product of a supernatural creator. There are many more explanatory options available, including the suggestion that God created life indirectly, by creating evolution (a position known as 'theistic evolution').

Alternatively, some scientists argue that nature's ability to evolve things (whether or not that ability is itself the product of design, as all theists believe) does not account for all of the relevant evidence, and that the theory of evolution is a partial truth that needs to be subsumed within a theory of 'intelligent design'.[9] If this growing minority of scholars is right, then discovering aliens would actually support the conclusion that God exists (and that he created life more than once). Either way, theists have no trouble admitting that intelligent life might exist out there.

Moreover, Schick attacks an unfairly weak characterization of his target. As we have already pointed out, the Bible neither confirms nor denies the existence of intelligent alien life forms. The Bible doesn't confirm or deny the existence of the telephone, but no one looks at their telephone and concludes that the Bible has been falsified.

Perhaps 'Small is Beautiful'

Many atheists suggest that SETI's emphasis on the enormity of space somehow undermines any belief in the special value of human beings. The picture of the cosmos developed by the ancient Greeks (principally Aristotle and Ptolemy) had Earth in the middle being circled by a series of nested, concentric spheres containing the planets and the stars. At first this model was a good fit with the available evidence. Over the years various observations were made that didn't fit this model, but which could be made to fit by adding circles within circles (called 'epicycles') in order to obtain ever more complex and accurate movements from the heavenly bodies. Eventually, astronomers like Copernicus (1473–1543) argued that the old model was needlessly complicated, and that it was simpler to suppose that the Earth and the other planets were orbiting the Sun. This shift, from a model with Earth at the centre to one with the Sun at the centre, is known as 'the Copernican revolution'.

Gregory Stock writes that: 'the special significance of humanity seemed clear to Western thinkers in the Middle Ages; Earth was at the centre of the universe.'[10] However, says Stock, 'The Copernican revolution shattered that notion, wrenching humanity from its exalted station and leaving it stranded on a peripheral planet circling one of many stars.'[11] However, the idea that the pre-Copernican cosmology gave humans significance by placing them in the centre of a small cosmos is misplaced. C.S. Lewis points out that medieval moralists recognised the Earth's cosmic insignificance, often referring to it when decrying human ambition.[12] In the pre-Copernican scheme of things, the centre of the universe was seen more as the dumping ground at the bottom, rather than the nerve-centre.[13] It is wrong to think of the Ptolemaic view regarding the Earth as a universal high-point which Copernicus reduced to insignificance.

The importance of a thing has nothing to do with its spatial position (is someone in the centre of the room more important than someone in the corner?), or size (is a man worth less than a tree?). Scientific descriptions of the universe are in principle incapable of ruling out notions of design, significance, or purpose. Besides, it seems that an appreciation of the size of creation at least cuts both ways, for:

> When one stares upward into a clear and dark night sky and out across the vast star fields of our galaxy, a sense of mystical astonishment is inevitable. When one thinks of how small our galaxy is in the larger scheme of things, even greater wonder is inspired.[14]

This sense of cosmic wonder motivates reflection upon the contingency, beauty and design of the heavens that has led many to conclude that there is a designer behind the cosmos.[15]

The Drake Equation

The question of whether aliens (monstrous or otherwise) actually exist can be broken down into a number of smaller, subsidiary questions. Some of these were organised into an equation by SETI researcher Frank Drake.[16] The 'Drake Equation' suggests that the number of detectable civilizations can be determined by multiplying the rate of formation for stars suitable for life, by the fraction of those stars with planets, by the fraction of planets suitable for life, by the fraction of planets where life arises, by the fraction of these on which intelligent life arises, by the fraction of these civilizations that will produce detectable signs of their existence, multiplied by the length of time for which such civilizations will produce detectable signs of their existence.[17] The answer people get out of this equation can depend more upon their philosophical assumptions than upon scientific evidence. For example, biologist Paul Ewald says: 'if there is life on other planets, natural selection *has to be* the fundamental organizing principle there.'[18] While theists can accept evolution as God's way of populating creation, there can be no '*has to be*' about it for anyone who believes in God.[19] Indeed, the Drake equation depends upon the assumption that life is caused by the inherent capacities of nature. It assumes that the whole 'atoms to people' theory of neo-Darwinian evolution is true. However, if the alternative theory of intelligent design is correct, this assumption is false.

Detecting Signs of Intelligence

SETI monitors millions of radio signals from space in the hope of detecting signs of intelligence. Some natural objects produce radio waves (e.g. pulsars).[20] Looking for signs of intelligence among all the naturally occurring signals is like looking for a needle in a haystack. To find that needle, researchers run the signals they detect through pattern-matching computers: 'So long as the signal doesn't match one of the preset patterns, it will pass through the pattern-matching sieve (and that even if it has an intelligent source). If, on the other hand, it does match one of these patterns, then ... the SETI researchers may have cause for celebration.'[21] What sort of pattern do SETI researchers look for? What sort of pattern is a reliable sign of intelligence? The movie *Contact* (based on the book by scientist Carl Sagan) dramatised the fictional discovery of the right sort of signal, a sequence representing the prime numbers from 2 to 101. The scientists in *Contact* took this signal as confirmation of alien life. Why?

Mathematician and philosopher William A. Dembski[22] argues that to reliably infer design on the basis of empirical evidence, we must establish two things: complexity and specification. His argument is easily understood by way of illustration: A long string of random letters drawn from a Scrabble bag would be complex without being specified (exhibiting a non *ad hoc* pattern). A short sequence of letters such as 'so' or 'the' drawn from the Scrabble bag would be specified (they mean something by the independently given rules of English) without being complex. In neither case is there any need to invoke design as an explanation (although both cases might actually be the product of design, they could also both be the result of chance). However, a long string of letters that formed a *Doctor Who* script would be both complex *and* specified, and would therefore require an explanation in terms of design. Likewise, the signal in *Contact* was both complex and specified, and this is what told the scientists that they had detected an alien civilization. It is this sort of 'complex, specified information' (CSI) that SETI needs to find if it is ever to prove that aliens exist.

According to intelligent design theory, this sort of pattern is found throughout nature. Hence design theorists have claimed that intelligent design can be scientifically inferred from many features of the universe, including:

- The fine-tuning of the laws of nature.[23]
- The fine-tuning of our cosmic habitat (e.g. the structure of our solar system).[24]
- The origin of life (e.g. the information-bearing structure of DNA).[25]

Let us briefly examine these three proposed 'signs of intelligence' in relation to *Doctor Who*.

A Cosmos Fine-Tuned for Life

Even a slight deviation from the basic physical laws of the cosmos would have produced a universe unable to support life. Life can only exist in a certain *very* unlikely kind of universe, and that's exactly the kind of universe in which we live. For example, the balance of matter and anti-matter 'had to be accurate to one part in ten billion for the universe to arise.'[26] If the strong nuclear force were 2 per cent weaker, protons and neutrons wouldn't stick together. If it were 0.3 per cent stronger, hydrogen (a crucial component of biological systems) could not exist.[27] Don N. Page calculates the odds against the formation of our universe at one in 10,000,000,000 to the power of 124![28] As British astronomer Sir Fred Hoyle complained: 'A common sense interpretation of the facts suggests that a superintellect has monkeyed with physics.'[29]

Douglas Adams, one-time *Doctor Who* script editor and author of *The Hitchhiker's Guide to the Galaxy*, thought he had a knockdown response to this 'fine-tuning' argument for design. He likened it to a puddle of water arguing that since the dip in the ground it inhabited seemed to fit it so well, the dip must have been created with its existence in mind: 'This is ... an interesting hole I find myself in – fits me rather neatly, doesn't it? In fact it fits me staggeringly well, must have been made to have me in it!'[30] While this analogy is a nice piece of humour, as a rebuttal of the fine-tuning argument it is flawed. Water fits any shape of hole – the fit between the hole and the water can be explained wholly by reference to the nature of water. However, life will not fit just any old environment. The fit between life and our cosmic environment cannot be explained wholly by reference to the nature of life.

The fact that we wouldn't be here if the universe were minutely different doesn't explain why our unlikely universe exists. Suppose you were up for execution by a practiced firing squad. Suppose the soldiers fire, but all miss. Would your relieved surprise be alleviated if I pointed out that you wouldn't be around to feel surprised if the soldiers had been on target? You might accept that you were simply the beneficiary of dumb luck, but isn't a better, more likely explanation that the soldiers missed on purpose? Likewise, cosmic fine-tuning could be dumb luck, but for many people it is a better explanation to say that it was set up that way on purpose.

Some people try to avoid this conclusion by suggesting the existence of a large number of universes, all with different laws. Indeed, *Doctor Who* embraces a 'many universes' cosmology. For example, the Doctor talks about 'all the universes' in 'The Invasion of Time' (1978). However, philosopher Stephen Clark comments:

> It is a mark of desperation that some atheistical materialists have chosen to believe in infinite arrays of universes ... rather than believe instead that this well-adapted world is founded on intelligence ... explaining away this world by saying that *all* worlds happen (which does not follow anyway merely from there being, we fantasise, an infinite array of worlds) ... destroys the basis of all explanation (since we could not, on those terms, be right to be surprised at anything).[31]

The best explanation of cosmic fine-tuning (an example of CSI) is that some intelligence took care to set up the physical laws of the universe so that they would produce a life-sustaining universe.

A Solar System Finely Tuned and Placed for Life

Doctor Who is full of Earth-like planets (many of which in classic *Doctor Who* look like quarries or sand-pits – often, indeed, the same quarries. Curious). However, scientific opinion suggests that there is probably only one planet for every thousand stars in the universe, and that the likelihood of other Earth-like planets capable of sustaining complex life is extremely poor: 'there was a time … when prominent astronomers seriously speculated about intelligent beings on the Moon, Mars, Venus, Jupiter, and even the Sun', write Gonzalez and Richards: 'Nowadays, thanks to our growing knowledge of these environments and the stringent requirements for life … Martians sound quaint … the other planets in the Solar System are not good candidates for life.'[32] The Ice Warriors may have come from Mars and menaced Patrick Troughton's Doctor, but subsequent scientific discoveries can give us the confidence to doubt any similar event in real life. The existence of planets beyond our solar system which are as hospitable to life as the ubiquitous quarry is unlikely. Peter Ward and Donald Browlee assert that only about 5 per cent or 6 per cent of examined stars have detectable planets.[33] They go on to point out that, although we can detect only gas giants (like Jupiter), of seventeen nearby stars with gas giants, all have orbits that would be disastrous, rather than helpful, for life on any smaller, rocky planets nearby. Therefore, it is extremely unlikely that any other planetary system resembles the one that we call home.

It's not just the solar system that is unusually 'just right', meeting the complex (unlikely) specification of conditions necessary for life. The galactic address of the solar system is also special. Gallifrey, the Doctor's home world, is probably: 'at the galactic core ... in Earth's Galaxy.'[34] Such a location is unpromising. There is a black hole at the centre of our galaxy (as in nearly every large galaxy nearby). Black holes are generally inactive, but whenever something gets near enough to be pulled in (as the Time Lord Omega was, according to 'The Three Doctors', 1973), everything in the vicinity is subjected to high levels of radiation. That's bad news for life. On the other hand, the spiral arms of the Milky Way are the main place where active star formation takes place, and that's bad for life as well, because of the high rate of supernova explosions. There is only 'a narrow safe zone where life-sustaining planets are possible.'[35] Earth is to be found in just such a zone, located between the Sagittarius and Perseus spiral arms. It seems that you couldn't find a better location for the Earth to sustain life if you tried.

The Origin of Life

In 'City of Death' (1979) the Doctor stops a time-travelling alien called Scaroth from preventing the destruction of his spaceship, because the explosion provided the energy that caused life to begin in the 'primal soup' on pre-historic Earth. In reality, the idea that life could arise from some 'warm little pond' of chemicals, as Darwin speculated, is scientifically suspect.[36] There is no evidence that such a 'soup' ever existed. Darwin's 'warm little pond' scenario for the origin of life is an unsubstantiated, atheistic 'just so' story. Moreover, as Walter L. Bradley reports, the origin of a system that is both rich in information and able to reproduce itself 'has absolutely stymied origin-of-life scientists.'[37]

Darwin thought that the world under the microscope was made up of simple jellies and crystals that could easily have formed at random. In fact, when we examine the chemical basis of life we find highly complex arrangements of matter that are specified by their biological functionality. According to Richard Dawkins: 'Complicated things have some quality, specifiable in advance, that is highly unlikely to have been acquired by random chance alone. In the case of living things, the quality that is specified in advance is ... the ability to propagate genes in reproduction.'[38] These complex systems cannot be explained by Darwin's theory of evolution by natural selection, for the simple reason that they must exist before anything can evolve. As Dawkins admits: '[For evolution to occur] you need raw materials that can self-replicate ... The *sine qua non* [that without which] ... is self-replication.'[39] In a letter to *Philosophy Now* magazine, noted philosopher Antony Flew discussed: 'the limits of the negative theological implications of Darwin's Theory of Evolution by Natural Selection.'[40] Flew noted that the theory cannot explain the origin of life which is capable of evolving, and observed: 'Probably Darwin himself believed that life was miraculously breathed into that primordial form of not always consistently reproducing life by God.'[41] Dawkins simply affirms that: 'Given enough time, anything is possible.'[42] But there simply isn't enough time to make a naturalistic origin of evolvable life plausible. Philosopher of science Stephen C. Meyer calculates: 'the probability of constructing a rather short, function protein at random [is] so small as to be effectively zero ... even given our multi-billion-year-old universe.'[43] Professor of Mathematics at Cardiff University, Chandra Wickramasinghe, and renowned Professor of Astronomy, Fred Hoyle, jointly conclude:

> The enormous information content of even the simplest living systems ... cannot in our view be generated by

what are often called 'natural' processes ... There is no way in which we can expect to avoid the need for information, no way in which we can simply get by with a bigger and better organic soup, as we ourselves hoped might be possible ... The correct position we think is ... an intelligence, which designed the biochemicals and gave rise to the origin of carbonaceous life ... This is tantamount to arguing that carbonaceous life was invented by noncarbonaceous intelligence.[44]

We Are Not Alone

In 'The Chase' (1965) Ian Chesterton finds a book in the TARDIS library called *Monsters from Outer Space*, which he considers 'a bit far fetched'. In the real world, belief in monsters from outer space is more than a bit far fetched. The evidence suggests that organic life (certainly intelligent life) is only found on Earth. If aliens do exist, they cannot be accounted for by the inherent capacities of nature alone. Moreover, the same method SETI uses to detect intelligence in radio signals actually detects signs of intelligence within the very fabric of nature. The fine-tuning of the cosmos, the galactic location and form of our solar system and the biochemical preconditions of evolution are all examples of specified complexity from which, on the basis of experience, we can reliably infer intelligent design. As Meyer writes: 'experience ... confirms that systems with large amounts of specified complexity ... invariably originate from an intelligent source.'[45] Hence if aliens do exist, it is only because they, like we, are here by design, and that there must be a designer who made us all for a purpose. In short, the evidence indicates that while we might well be alone in one sense, we are far from being alone in quite another.

In 'Aliens of London' the Doctor described the moment of humanity's first proper contact with an alien species as being the point where 'the human race finally grows up'. Perhaps it could be argued that engagement with our designer is a more significant rite of passage for each of us.

Notes

1 cf. www.seti-inst.edu/
2 news.bbc.co.uk/1/hi/sci/tech/254277.stm.
3 www.prnewswire.com/cgi-bin/storiespl?ACCT=109&STORY=/www/story/05-262005/0003691868&EDATE=.
4 *Free Inquiry*, Summer 2000, p. 32.
5 According to the 2005 *National Geographic Channel* poll: 'People who are regular churchgoers are less-likely to believe in life on other planets compared to non-churchgoers, 46% vs. 70%.'
6 Jill Tarter, 'SETI and the Religions of Extraterrestrials', *Free Inquiry*, Summer 2000, p. 34.
7 Theodore Schick, 'When Humanists Meet E.T', *Free Inquiry*, Summer 2000, p. 36.
8 Maurice Chittenden, 'Bishops put their faith in aliens' at www.virtuallystrange.net/ufo/updates/1998/mar/m25-003.shtml.
9 cf. Mark Hartwig, 'Frequently Asked Questions About Intelligent Design Theory' at www.arn.org/id_faq.htm; Peter S. Williams, 'Intelligent Design Theory – An Overview' at www.arn.org/docs/williams/pw_idtheoryoverview.htm#_edn188; Thomas Woodward, *Doubts About Darwin: A History of Intelligent Design* (Baker, 2003).
10 Gregory Stock, *Redesigning Humans* (Profile, 2002), p. 174.
11 Gregory Stock, *Redesigning Humans*, p. 175.
12 See, for example, C.S. Lewis, *The Discarded Image* (Cambridge University Press, 1994), p. 26.

[13] See Guillermo Gonzalez & Jay W. Richards, *The Privileged Planet* (Regnery, 2004), pp. 226 and 228.

[14] Donald E. Tarter, 'Looking for God and Space Aliens', *Free Inquiry*, Summer 2000, p. 39.

[15] cf. Michael J. Behe, William A. Dembski and Stephen C. Meyer, *Science and Evidence for Design in the Universe* (Ignatius, 2000); Thomas Dubay, *The Evidential Power of Beauty* (Ignatius, 1999); Keith Ward, *God, Chance & Necessity* (OneWorld, 1996).

[16] cf. www.activemind.com/Mysterious/Topics/SETI/biography_drake.html.

[17] That is: $N = R^* \times Fp \times Ne \times Fl \times Fi \times Fc \times L$.

[18] Paul Ewald, quoted by Phillip E. Johnson, 'The Intelligent Design Movement', in William A. Dembski & James M. Kushner (eds.), *Signs of Intelligence* (Brazos Press, 2001), p. 30, our emphasis.

[19] cf. Alvin Plantinga, 'When Faith and Reason Clash: Evolution and the Bible' at www.asa3.org/ASA/dialogues/Faith-reason/CRS9-91Plantinga1.html; Alvin Plantinga, 'Methodological Naturalism?' at http://id-www.ucsb.edu/fscf/library/plantinga/mn/home.html.

[20] When pulsars were discovered the scientists involved thought that perhaps they had discovered aliens. However, the repetitive signal from a pulsar lacks the complexity that requires a 'design' explanation.

[21] William A. Dembski, 'Science & Design' at www.arn.org/ftissues/ft9810/articles/dembski.html.

[22] cf. www.arn.org/dembski/wdhome.htm.

[23] cf. Walter L. Bradley, 'The Designed "Just So" Universe at www.leaderu.com/offices/bradley/docs/universe.html; William Lane Craig, 'Review: The Design Inference' at www.leaderu.com/offices/billcraig/docs/design.html.

[24] Hugh Ross, 'Probability for Life On Earth' at www.reasons.org/resources/apologetics/design_evidences/200404_probabilities_for_life_on_earth.shtml; Guillermo Gonzalez & Jay W. Richards, *The Privileged Planet: How Our Place in the Cosmos Is Designed for Discovery* (Regnery, 2004).

[25] Stephen C. Meyer, 'DNA and Other Designs' at www.arn.org/docs/meyer/sm_dnaotherdesigns.htm.

[26] J.P. Moreland, *Scaling the Secular City* (Baker, 1987).

[27] cf. Jimmy H. Davies and Harry L. Poe, *Designer Universe* (Broadman & Holman, 2002), p. 85.

[28] Quoted by L. Stafford Betty and Bruce Cordell, 'The Anthropic Teleological Argument', *International Philosophical Quarterly* 27, No. 4 (December 1987).

[29] Fred Hoyle, quoted in Fred Hereen, *Show Me God* (Search Light, 1995), p. 179.

[30] Douglas Adams, *The Salmon of Doubt* (Pan, 2003), p. 131.

[31] Stephen R. L. Clark, *God, Religion and Reality* (SPCK, 1998), p. 106.

[32] Guillermo Gonzalez & Jay W. Richards, *The Privileged Planet* (Regnery, 2004), pp. 152 and 252.

[33] Peter Ward & Donald Brownlee, *Rare Earth* (Springer-Verlag, 2000), p. 268.

[34] Paul Cornell, Martin Day & Keith Topping, *The Discontinuity Guide* (MonkeyBrain, 2004), p. 126.

[35] Guillermo Gonzalez, in Lee Strobel, *The Case for a Creator* (Zondervan, 2004) p. 170.

[36] cf. Stephen C. Meyer, 'DNA & Other Designs' (*First Things* 102, April 1, 2000) at www.arn.org/docs/meyer/sm_dnaotherdesigns.htm; Gordon C. Mills, Malcolm Lancaster & Walter L. Bradley, 'Origin of Life & Evolution in Biology Textbooks: A Critique' (*The American Biology Teacher*, Volume 55, No. 2, February 1993, 78–83) at www.arn.org/docs/mills/gm_originoflifeandevolution.htm.

[37] Walter L. Bradley, in Lee Strobel, *The Case for Faith* (Zondervan, 2000), p. 100.

[38] Richard Dawkins, *The Blind Watchmaker* (Penguin, 1990), p. 9.

[39] Richard Dawkins, 'Darwin's Dangerous Disciple' at www.skeptic.com/03.4.miele-dawkins-iv.html.

[40] Antony Flew, *Philosophy Now*, Issue 47, August/September 2004, p. 22.

[41] Antony Flew, *Philosophy Now*, Issue 47.

[42] Dawkins, *The Blind Watchmaker* (Penguin, 1990), p. 139.

[43] Stephen C. Meyer, "Word Games', in William A. Dembski & James M. Kushner (eds.), *Signs of Intelligence* (Brazos, 2001), p. 110.

[44] Fred Hoyle & Chandra Wickramasinghe, *Evolution from Space* (Dent, 1981), pp. 24–148.

[45] Stephen C. Meyer, 'The Origin of Biological Information and the Higher Taxonomic Categories', *Proceedings of the Biological Society of Washington* (Volume 117, No. 2, 2004, pp. 213–239).

12. Conclusion: The Strands of Time

This is who I am, right here right now, all right? All that counts is here and now, and this is me.
The Doctor in 'The End of the World'

In 2002, the British Patent Office ruled that the BBC should hold the copyright of the TARDIS' blue police box design, on the basis that despite there still being 237 authentic police boxes in existence (put to more mundane use as coffee stalls and the like, rather than as a temporary lock-up for criminals), most people are more likely to associate them with *Doctor Who*.[1] The fact that the otherwise long-forgotten police boxes were a common sight on our streets when the TARDIS made its first appearance reflects the extraordinary longevity of the show.

Since *Doctor Who* was first broadcast on BBC television, there have been seven British Prime Ministers and eight American Presidents;[2] decimal currency has been introduced to Britain and the Common Market has become first the EEC and now the European Community. Other TV shows have come and gone with *Coronation Street*[3] the only current show that can lay claim to a longer history on British television. What is it about *Doctor Who* that has made it such a popular and enduring show?

Tom Baker recalls meeting a man in the street who recognised him from his role as the Doctor:

> He said, 'You know, when I was a kid, I was in care in North Wales. You know, on Saturday night you made it really great.' And as he said that, I could see he was moved remembering his childhood. I went to speak to him and he couldn't speak, he just did that [holds up hand] and he was gone. And I looked and saw him weaving down the road. I realised the immense power of nostalgia.[4]

Doctor Who certainly has a powerful nostalgic power for those of us who watched the show in the golden days, but so do countless other programmes which have never lasted as long or been revived so successfully. What was it about *Doctor Who* that marks it out from other TV shows?

True Stories

Doctor Who has always had a uniquely versatile format at the very core of the show. Original producer Verity Lambert has commented that 'it was such a flexible format, you could do almost anything you wanted.'[5] Each adventure could be set somewhere different, with the whole of time and space available as a canvas for the writers to set their work against. The presence of a core of regular characters provided an element of consistency to anchor the wide-ranging series. The person of the Doctor ensures a sense of mystery and enigma, while his regularly updated collection of companions provided characters the audience find easier to identify with than a 900-year-old Time Lord.

The Doctor's never-ending battle against evil is also central to the programme's appeal. Every week, the Doctor discovers an evil plot of some kind, and does whatever he has to in order to prevent it. While some critics have complained about the levels of violence in the programme, its defenders have often countered by pointing out that good always triumphs in the end. Paul Cornell, writer of 'Father's Day', remembers the impact that this had on him as a child watching the programme:

> I was quite surprised when the Doctor won. And that surprise did something big to my insides. It kind of exorcised something, it made things better, and that was kind of important to me.[6]

Doctor Who provides children with the opportunity to be scared in safety. The appeal is not dissimilar to a Ghost Train ride at a fun fair – we can scream and hide behind the sofa, but at the same time we know it isn't real. And good always wins. The universe that *Doctor Who* lives in is one where bad things happen, but the forces of good ultimately come out on top – precisely the same type of universe that Christians believe in. As we suggested in Chapter 7, *Doctor Who* is a 'drama of reassurance' which touches something deeply embedded in our human experience. Jane Trantor, the BBC executive who commissioned the 2005 series of *Doctor Who*:

> It's quite difficult to find escapist fantasy dramas that actually feel as if they've got some kind of root in our lives, in the way we live now. And the whole concept of *Doctor Who* allows us to do that week after week after week.[7]

Although *Doctor Who* features invented monsters (Daleks and Draconians, Slitheen and Sontarans), although it features a space and time ship that is bigger on the inside than on the outside and stars a centuries-old leading man who completely regenerates into a new body from time to time, although much of the show is pure fantasy, nevertheless *Doctor Who* rings true to us.

Technological Revolution

The challenge for Russell T. Davies and the team working on the 2005 series of *Doctor Who* was how to tap into all the things that had made the old show great, while also bringing it up to date for a new century and a new audience. Executive producer Mal Young saw Davies as having the right abilities to complete this revision of the format:

> If it gets in the way of a good story and taking the show forward, it has to be pushed to one side. He gets the balance right I think. He knows what to take and what to leave behind.[8]

The basic format of a man who travels in time and space having adventures was to be unchanged, and the principle of producing a pre-watershed family show was quickly agreed. But there were two significant changes that were to be made.

First of all, the show was able to spend money on special effects like never before. For all the ingenuity of the design teams on the original show, and for all the genuinely impressive effects that were achieved, there were always occasions when time and resources were lacking, resulting in something making it onto the screen which really didn't convince. Quality varied wildly from year to year, episode to episode, and even from scene to scene. As we suggested in Chapter 2, our more sophisticated modern eyes are quick to brand as unconvincing things which were breathtakingly impressive thirty or more years ago. For example, 'The Ark In Space' (1975) features a monster costume consisting of an actor crawling around while wrapped in bubblewrap which has been painted green. Now it looks quite laughable; back then bubblewrap was a brand new and unfamiliar material, and we were scared.

But now all that has changed. Thanks to the wonders of CGI, and a BBC willing to back *Doctor Who* with a serious budget, the 2005 series features the most impressive special effects ever seen on a home-grown British TV series, and certainly in a similar league to American shows such as *Buffy the Vampire Slayer* and the newer entries to the *Star Trek* franchise. Andrew Cartmel has described how in the late 1980s he was reduced to avoiding non-humanoid monsters for fear of what fresh depths the design department would sink to.[9] It is almost unthinkable that a character like Cassandra would have made it past initial discussions in such an environment. The new technical possibilities have made the show more convincing than ever before.

Coming of Age

Secondly, while a commitment to story over visuals remains, there is also a new maturity to the writing on the 2005 show. The long period between the demise of McCoy's Doctor and the appearance of Eccleston's witnessed the development of *Doctor Who* fan fiction, and the appearance of a large number of new *Doctor*

Who stories in the media of novels and audio adventures. This is significant in two ways. First of all, because these stories frequently offered more depth than the classic TV show was always able to provide, and secondly because all of the writers of the 2005 series (Russell T. Davies included) had previously authored at least one story in either novel or audio form. Paul Cornell comments on the difference between the *Doctor Who* that he watched as a child and the 2005 version:

> Way back when it was the children's teatime show that adults adore it was always more of a Saturday afternoon serial. You didn't worry about the consequences of violent action too much, you just wanted to get to the next adventure, and quite right too. These days I think we are looking for a more thoughtful approach to the consequences of that action and this whole new series is more emotionally committed.[10]

That the 2005 series even found room to make a Dalek sympathetic (in 'Dalek') shows the extent of that emotional commitment. Cornell's own episode 'Father's Day' is a fine example of how the new show is unafraid to play to an adult audience just as much as to the kids. The official BBC *Doctor Who* website graded each episode with a 'fear forecast', which was based on allowing a panel of children to watch the show with their parents and to have their reactions observed. In the fear forecast report for 'Father's Day', it is notable that there are several moments when the children are unmoved, but their parents are in tears.[11] Actor Simon Pegg sums up the relationship of the 2005 *Doctor Who* to the previous versions of the show:

> It feels a lot like the show's grown up but without losing any of its original charm.[12]

Russell T. Davies and his team have successfully built on the foundations of the show's heritage, but also created something more substantial and more satisfying, both intellectually and emotionally.

Mankind Stands Tall

There are two basic truths that can be asserted about *Doctor Who*. First, it is a show that embraces humanity, and secondly that it is a hugely optimistic show. These two truths are inextricably interconnected throughout the programme. For all of the Doctor's complaints about 'you lot ...' and for all his 'stupid ape' comments, the show has a great deal of positive comment to make about humanity.

Even in the very first episode of the 2005 series, the Doctor pleads on our behalf with the Nestene Consciousness, telling it that 'these stupid little people have only just learned how to walk, but they're capable of so much more'. Similarly in 'The End of the World' he tells Rose:

> You lot, you spend all your time thinking about dying. Like you're going to get killed by eggs, or beef, or global warming or asteroids. But you never take time to imagine the impossible, that maybe you survive.

Humanity has a great and glorious future, according to the Doctor. He describes our first official contact with an alien race as the point 'when the human race finally grows up', the thing that enables us to 'expand'. According to *Doctor Who* humanity's future will see us spreading ourselves across the galaxies, mixing with alien races and interbreeding with them to become the most wide-ranging and important species in the Universe.

And in almost every episode of the series, there is at least one instance of a human character showing a willingness to sacrifice their own life for the sake of others. If you include Jabe (admittedly a tree, but her roots – excuse the pun – on Earth and her humanoid appearance justify her presence in this list), then only 'Rose' and 'Boom Town' stand as episodes lacking in such an act. From Gwyneth in 'The Unquiet Dead' to the volunteers defending the Games Station in 'Parting of the Ways', noble self-sacrifice shows the best side of human nature time and time again. Sometimes, as with Rose's Dad or the controller in 'Bad Wolf', the sacrifice is absolutely necessary. Other instances, such as De Maggio's attempt to hold off the Dalek on the stairs in 'Dalek' are futile, but no less admirable for that.

The optimism of the show also shines through in one simple fact: the Doctor always wins. Despite all the schemes and plots of his foes, despite sometimes not even having a plan, (as he admits to Rose in 'Father's Day' and to the Daleks in 'Parting of the Ways'), he still manages to come out on top. Sometimes that victory has a bitter-sweet feel to it, or comes at a terrible cost, but the Doctor always wins.

The Toleration Game

Thematically, there are a number of tensions that underpin *Doctor Who*. The concept of tolerance is crucial to both the show and its central character, and yet in every single adventure the Doctor acts decisively, refusing to tolerate the schemes of whichever foe he finds himself pitted against. He urges Rose to have a great life, but offers two distinct lines of thought as to what constitutes a great life.

First of all, a great life is one of open-minded enquiry, of broadening horizons. Rose is told to get used to the new morality or go home, Dickens is told that he has more to learn, Cathica is mocked for her lack of curiosity, then admired for overcoming her conditioning and challenging the status quo on Satellite Five.

But it is also clear that tolerance has its limits. When others are being intolerant, oppressing the weak and seeking to curtail liberty and freedom, the Doctor is quick to act against them, and quick to praise others who do the same. In 'The Empty Child' the Doctor's praise of humanity (and in particular, it seems from this example, the British) is focused on precisely this tendency:

> 1941. Right now, not very far from here the German war machine is rolling up the map of Europe. Country after country falling like dominoes. Nothing can stop it, nothing. Until one tiny, damp little island says, 'No. No, not here.' A mouse in front of a lion. You're amazing, the lot of you. I don't know what you do to Hitler, but you frighten the hell out of me. Off you go then, do what you've got to do, save the world.

Tolerance is a good thing in *Doctor Who*, but sometimes principles demand that we make a stand against things. Not to do so would be a failure to live the great life that the Doctor demands of Rose and of us.

Although, as we have already noted, these two elements are held in tension to each other, this does not mean that they are mutually contradictory. The concept of tolerance is one that is primarily about our individual development and growth – what we should be like in and of ourselves, according to the Doctor. The concept of making a stand and opposing things that are wrong is primarily about how we relate to the society in which we find ourselves. In the context of *Doctor Who*, it could be argued that the second factor only comes into play when the Doctor encounters someone (or something) acting in a way that shows disregard for the first. Even the Doctor's decisive and, some might say, intolerant actions are always intended to promote tolerant and open-minded pursuit of knowledge and liberty. Principles are not a bad thing in the Doctor's worldview, but they should be non-dogmatic and open to questioning and re-examination. Anything less than that leads us down the road to Dalek-like oppression and hatred. Nevertheless, as we suggest in Chapters 8 and 10, in the naturalistic worldview suggested by *Doctor Who*, there can be no objective basis for the very principles that we are urged to stand for.

Open-Minded Faith

Traditionally, *Doctor Who* has tended to cast those who believe in religion and the spiritual dimension of life as belonging to the legions of the closed-minded that the Doctor opposes at every opportunity. However, it can be argued that over the course of his nine generations so far, he is more often pitted against foes who are motivated by hard-headed scientific materialism. Cybermen and Daleks (at least, prior to the latter's 'Parting of the Ways' zealotry) only scratch the surface of this recurring trend. If religion stands accused of blazing a trail for the narrow-minded and intolerant, then scientism stands equally accused by the good Doctor. As we argue in Chapter 9, this reflects the fact that science and religion are not implacably opposed to each other. Each of them present dangers when abused and misrepresented, but each at their best are also powerful aids in our search for truth, understanding and personal growth. It may be that some readers of this book will find themselves reacting against the Christian faith of the authors, and the expression of it in a book about a programme like *Doctor Who*. But isn't it likely that the Doctor would argue that such a reaction – as opposed to dealing intelligently with the arguments and reasons presented – is precisely the kind of intolerance that he travels the universe in order to counter?

Time's Saviour

In Chapter 2 we pointed out the large number of parallels between the Doctor and Jesus. Sometimes – as in *Doctor Who: The Movie* (1996) the parallels are so explicit as to be undeniably intentional. At other times they are more likely to be coincidental, simply the result of writers developing the character in the way that best suits the story. It is certainly noticeable that Eccleston's Doctor makes frequent reference to 'saving the world' – rebuking the Slitheen for farting while he attempts to do so ('Aliens of London'); worrying that he might lose Rose in the process ('World War Three'); promising to try to save Stuart and Sarah ('Father's Day'); and threatening the Daleks with the promise that he will save the Earth and then wipe them out of the sky ('Bad Wolf'). Death may be, as Clive says in 'Rose', the Doctor's constant companion, but salvation seems to be his constant thought.

As we explained in Chapter 6, Christians believe that the only hope of defeating the final enemy, death, is to be found in Jesus. Russell T. Davies, talking specifically about the scene in 'Parting of the Ways' where the Daleks descend to floor zero and kill all of the people who refused to volunteer for Captain Jack's defence force, says this:

> There are great moments in *Doctor Who* where there's no hope, where it's very bleak. The Doctor is your hope, and Rose. They are your beacons of hope throughout the whole series. If they're not there – and the Doctor hasn't even been to floor zero – then you're dead.[13]

The Doctor (and his companions) are the embodiment of hope in *Doctor Who*, just as Jesus is the embodiment of hope in the Christian faith. The powerful desire to escape death lies at the heart of our human nature, and the repeated appearance of death in *Doctor Who* is a reflection of this. We all know that one day we must face death. More than this, consciously or subconsciously, we all yearn for a hope that will endure beyond it. The Doctor is a personification of this yearning, albeit an imperfect one. The Doctor cannot prevent every death and the most he can do is snatch a few from death's jaws and enable them to go on living for a time. This is an imperfect reflection of the Christian belief in a God who dies in our place in order to defeat death forever. The best that the Doctor can manage is summed up in his soul stirring exclamation towards the end of 'The Doctor Dances':

> Oh come on, give me a day like this. Give me this one . . . Everybody lives, Rose. Just this once, everybody lives.

The reason this scene stirs us so powerfully is that it goes right to the heart of one of humanity's most basic needs: the desire to escape death. Where the Doctor gives us a glimpse of partial victory, Christians believe that Jesus holds out the real deal. Indeed, the Doctor's desire to save is expressed in the form of an address, a prayer even, to some power beyond his own.

Personal Contact

But perhaps the most significant parallel between the Doctor and Jesus is the effect the Doctor has on the people around him. Billie Piper has commented that Rose 'understands her existence a whole lot more, having met the Doctor'.[14] What would Rose and Jack's lives have been like if they had never encountered the Doctor? It is unlikely that Rose would have lived anything other than the mundane life of work, chips and bed that the Doctor describes in 'Rose' (although she would have needed to find a new job, even if she never discovered how Hendrik's burned down). Jack would probably have carried on pulling scams to con the Time Agents. It is highly unlikely that either of them would have put themselves into situations where they were risking everything for the sake of others.

Quite apart from the impression the Doctor makes on Rose and Jack, there is a string of other characters in the 2005 series who find their lives transformed after crossing paths with the wandering Time Lord. Charles Dickens gains a new lease of life and a renewed intellectual excitement; Harriet Jones is transformed from a humble and unimportant backbench MP to a great and courageous leader; Cathica learns how to ask questions rather than meekly accept whatever is put in front of her. Even Margaret Slitheen is given the chance of a fresh start, literally being born (or hatched) again, although we get no indication of how she uses her second chance of a life. Whether someone encounters the Doctor over a prolonged period of time (like Rose) or briefly (like Harriet Jones), the impact on those who do not close their mind to him is profound.

Encountering Jesus can have a similar impact. One of the implications of Jesus' victory over death is, according to Christians, that he is alive today. Christian faith is not just a set of intellectual things to believe, it is a relationship with a real person. Clearly, a book such as this is not the place for personal testimony about such life-changing encounters, but it is important to point out that like Jesus, the Doctor identifies his own mission in terms of 'saving the world', and that both Jesus and the Doctor demonstrate a profound impact on their followers.

Back For Good

Doctor Who is extraordinarily successful because, as executive producer Mal Young says, 'through his eyes we question our society'.[15] It reflects our own image back to us, showing us both the best and the worst of humanity. More than that, it suggests that in order for us to live great lives – to live up to the best, rather than sink down to the worst – we need to take responsibility. We need to be willing to stand against injustice and oppression rather than lie down and give up. *Doctor Who* tells us that the way we live our lives does matter. It gives us reassurance that whatever terrors the universe may throw at us, we are able to withstand them. More than that, it tells us that we are not alone in a harsh and unfriendly universe – help is at hand. It tells us that there is a difference between good and evil, and that the forces of good can win.

These are huge, comforting claims. Perhaps the reason that they, and *Doctor Who*, resonate so powerfully within us is that we were made that way. Perhaps because we do live in a universe where good triumphs over evil and where we are not left alone, but can expect help from a saviour who will transform our lives. Christians find the ultimate sense of meaning and purpose in an obedient relationship with God. *Doctor Who* suggests that ultimate meaning is to be found in open-minded discovery and exploration. The two are by no means mutually exclusive.

Many long-standing fans were excited by the news that *Doctor Who* was returning to our screens in 2005, and delighted with the results once it did so. Many new fans who had never seen the old versions of the show have now discovered the delights of one man and his old blue Police Box. At the time of writing we don't know what David Tennant's Doctor, weird new teeth and all, will be like. What we do know is that the Doctor will continue to oppose evil and protect the helpless wherever he goes, and that it will be fantastic.

Notes

[1] Joe Boyle, 'New Doctor, same old Tardises', news.bbc. co.uk/1/hi/uk/4380929.stm.

[2] Prime Ministers: Home, Wilson (twice), Heath, Callaghan, Thatcher, Major, Blair. Presidents: Johnson, Nixon, Ford, Carter, Reagan, George Bush, Clinton, George W. Bush.

[3] The first episode of *Coronation Street* was broadcast by ITV on Friday 9 December 1960.

[4] Tom Baker, *Doctor Who Confidential: The World of Who* (BBC3, first broadcast 11 June 2005).

[5] Verity Lambert, *The Story of Doctor Who* (BBC2, first broadcast as part of '*Doctor Who* Night', Saturday 19 March 2005).

[6] Paul Cornell, in Phil Creighton 'Thrills and chills for all the family', *Baptist Times*, 19 May 2005.

7   Jane Trantor, *Project Who* (BBC Audiobooks, 2005).

8   Mal Young, *Project Who*.

9   Andrew Cartmel, *Script Doctor: The Inside Story of Doctor Who: 1986–89* (Reynolds and Hearn, 2005), p.118, p. 119, p. 137.

10 Paul Cornell, in Phil Creighton 'Thrills and chills for all the family'.

11 www.bbc.co.uk/doctorwho/news/cult/news/drwho/2005/05/14/19245.shtml.

12 Simon Pegg, quoted on *Doctor Who: The Ultimate Guide* (BBC1, first broadcast 18 June 2005).

13 Russell T. Davies, *Doctor Who Confidential: The Last Battle* (BBC3, first broadcast 18 June 2005).

14 Billie Piper, *Doctor Who Confidential: I Get A Side-kick Out Of You* (BBC3, first broadcast 16 April 2005).

15 Mal Young, *Project Who*.

Appendix 1:
Who's Who in New *Who*

A Glossary of characters, places and items in the 2005 series of *Doctor Who*

In view of the number of characters whose surnames are never revealed, all characters are listed in alphabetical order by their forenames. Where no forename is known, or where the surname is the usual term of address, they are listed by surname.

Adam: A young Englishman working for Henry van Statten until joining the Doctor and Rose in their travels. On his first adventure he travels almost 200,000 years into the future and attempts to steal technological secrets from Satellite Five. Furious, the Doctor takes him home and leaves him there. As a result of his greed, Adam is left with a huge biochip in his head, which activates whenever anyone clicks their fingers. The Doctor warns him that he must live an average life and avoid attracting attention, because if anyone discovers his implant, Adam is likely to be dissected.

Adherents of the Repeated Meme: Stooges of Cassandra in her attempt to sabotage the party at the end of the world. Their name is a reference to Richard Dawkins' concept of the meme – just because an idea is accepted and passed on from generation to generation, it doesn't mean that it's true, only that it is 'catchy'. Dawkins argues that such ideas are empty and meaningless, hence the disappearance of the Adherents when challenged by the Doctor.

Agorax: Contestant on *The Weakest Link*.

Albion Hospital: Location where the surgically altered pig/alien hybrid is taken in 'Aliens of London'. Also the hospital where Doctor Constantine works with the strangely infected patients in 'The Empty Child' and 'The Doctor Dances'. Albion is an ancient Celtic name for Britain.

Alexander Graham Bell: Inventor of the telephone. In the first ever phone call, he said, 'Watson, come here. I need you.' This phrase is heard on both Rose's and Sonny Hoskins' mobile phones during 'Father's Day' as time becomes contaminated.

Algy: Army officer friend of Jack Harkness. Jack says that Rose isn't likely to be his type.

Andrew Marr: Political editor at BBC television (2000–2005), who makes several cameo appearances in 'Aliens of London' and 'World War Three', commenting on the unlikely public figures who are arriving at 10 Downing Street.

Anne Droid: Robotic host of *The Weakest Link* on the Games Station. Modelled on real *Weakest Link* presenter Anne Robinson, who provided the voice of Anne Droid. Anne Droid's finest hour was disintegrating one of the Daleks during the final defence of the Games Station

– almost as satisfying a sight as the remaining Daleks exterminating Anne Droid immediately afterwards.

Antiplastic: The Doctor has a test tube full of blue liquid antiplastic, which he intends to use on the Nestene Consciousness if it won't leave Earth quietly. When he is grabbed by the Autons (which is probably as painful as it sounds) all looks lost until Rose swings in to knock the antiplastic into the vat containing the Nestene Consciousness.

Asquith, General: A senior officer in the British Army. He becomes concerned by Joseph Green's inappropriate behaviour, and when he attempts to relieve him of command is killed and replaced by the Slitheen.

Autons: Plastic shop-window dummies who are controlled by the Nestene Consciousness. They come equipped with concealed guns in their hands.

Bad Wolf: Phrase which haunts the Doctor from 'The End of the World' onwards. Most episodes in the series feature at least one reference to 'Bad Wolf', ranging from the subtle (grafitti scrawled on a flyposter in 'Father's Day') to the obvious (Bad Wolf written large on the side of the TARDIS in 'Aliens of London'). The Doctor first comments on it in 'Boom Town', when he asks Margaret Slitheen why she chose Blaidd Drwg as a name for the power plant. Eventually the truth emerges in 'Parting of the Ways': Bad Wolf is not a warning to the Doctor and Rose, it is a message from Rose to herself, telling her not to give up trying to get back to the Doctor. After she has looked into the heart of the TARDIS, she gains the ability to manipulate the fabric of time and space and to control life and death.

Barcelona: A planet where the dogs have no noses. The Doctor talks about taking Rose there shortly before he regenerates.

Bear With Me: TV show broadcast by the Games Station. Inexplicably, the Doctor likes this one. The celebrity special was particularly funny when the bear got in the bath, apparently.

Bev: A bridesmaid at Stuart and Sarah's wedding in 'Father's Day'.

Big Issue: Magazine sold to support the homeless in most major towns and cities in the UK. A *Big Issue* vendor is seen when the Doctor brings Rose back to Earth at the conclusion to 'The End of the World' – ironically given the Doctor's status as a homeless wanderer in time and space.

Blaidd Drwg: The name of the unsafe nuclear power station that Margaret Blaine is overseeing the construction of in 'Boom Town'. It is also Welsh for 'Bad Wolf', as the Doctor realises. See *Bad Wolf*.

Blon Fel Fotch Pasameer-Day Slitheen: The full name of the member of the Slitheen family who survives the destruction of 10 Downing Street. See *Margaret Blaine/ Slitheen*.

Britney Spears: Her song *Toxic* is played at the party at the end of the world. It is described by Cassandra as a 'classic ballad'. It was a number one hit in the UK in March 2004.

Broff: Contestant on *The Weakest Link*. He attempts to run away rather than completing the quiz, and is disintegrated by Anne Droid. He voted for Rose.

Brothers Hopp-Pyleen, The: Guests at the party at the end of the world. They are introduced as the inventors and copyright holders of Hyposlip travel systems.

Buffalo: The Doctor's password for the UNIT website.

Cal 'Spark Plug' MacNannovich: A cybernetic hyperstar, apparently. Cal is a guest on Platform One for the destruction of the world.

Call My Bluff: TV show broadcast on the Games Station. Lynda says it is played 'with real guns'. The original show was broadcast by the BBC from 1965, with the original host Robert Robinson being replaced by Bob Holness when it was revived in 1996.

Caroline: Clive's wife. When her son answers the door to Rose, Caroline is amazed to discover that a woman has been reading her husband's website. Caroline survives the Auton killing spree in the shopping centre together with their son.

Cassandra: The last human being, and the evil genius behind the plan to sabotage the party at the end of the world. Cassandra is in fact a disembodied brain, connected to a single stretched piece of skin with a face. She dismisses humans who have interbred with alien races as 'mongrels'. Bases her claims to pure-bred status on having the last two humans born on Earth and buried on Earth as her parents, but doesn't regard her hundreds of surgical operations as affecting this purity. When the Doctor teleports her back to Platform One to face the music, Cassandra dries out in the heat and is killed when her face splits apart. Dismissed by Rose as 'a bitchy trampoline'.

Cathica: An employee of Satellite Five in 'The Long Game'. Initially disparaged by the Doctor for not asking any questions, she begins to challenge the assumptions of life in the fast lane of newsgathering and plays a crucial role in overthrowing the Jagrafess.

Cathy Salt: Inquisitive journalist in 'Boom Town', whose life is spared by Margaret Slitheen once she reveals that she is pregnant.

Channel 44000: Broadcasters of the *Big Brother* show that features the Doctor – briefly – as a contestant.

Charles Dickens: The Victorian novelist, whose public reading is interrupted first by one of the Gelth and then by the Doctor and Rose. Dickens overcomes his avowed disbelief in supernatural fantasies and becomes convinced that the Doctor has shown him what the world is really like. As the Doctor tells Rose, he dies in 1870 (9 June, to be precise), some six months after the events of 'The Unquiet Dead', and so was unable to incorporate the Gelth into his final, unfinished novel, *The Mystery of Edwin Drood*.

Chicken, Mr: In 1730 Mr Chicken lived on the future site of 10 Downing Street. In 'World War Three' the Doctor says 'he was a nice man'.

Chula: Species who made the medical pod that caused all the trouble in 'The Empty Child' and 'The Doctor Dances'. Their nanogenes heal Rose's hands, and threaten to reprogram the DNA of the entire human race.

City State of Binding Light: Their ambassadors attend the party at the destruction of Earth on Platform One.

Clavadoe: A month in the pantraffic calendar. It doesn't come after Hoob.

Cleaver, Mr: Scientific advisor who pleads with Margaret Blaine to abandon the Blaidd Drwg project because the power plant is hopelessly unsafe. His fatal mistake was in telling her that he hadn't mentioned his findings to anyone else.

Clive: Runs a website about the Doctor's many appearances on Earth. The first person to die onscreen in the 2005 series of *Doctor Who*.

Clive's son: Dismisses those interested in his Dad's theories as 'nutters'. Survives the Auton killing spree along with his mother, Caroline.

Colleen: Contestant on *The Weakest Link*.

Commander: Foolishly ignores the Doctor's advice in 'Dalek', and claims to know 'how to fight one single tin robot'. He dies along with many of the men under his command.

Compact Laser Deluxe: Jack's sonic gun, hidden about his person (you really don't want to know where) which he uses to escape from Trine-e and Zu-zana.

Constantine, Doctor: A senior doctor at Albion Hospital in 'The Empty Child' and 'The Doctor Dances'.

Constantine stays with the patients to the bitter end, and is praised by the Doctor as 'the constant Doctor'. Shows a wry wit when asked to explain how a woman who came into the hospital with one leg now has two: 'There is a war on – could you have miscounted?'

Controller: Taken by the Daleks at the age of five to run the Games Station. She secretly Trans-Mats the Doctor, Rose and Jack into the games in order to get them on board the Games Station without the Daleks detecting them – they monitor the space station, but don't watch the games themselves. Once her betrayal is discovered the Daleks transport her to one of their ships. The Controller remains defiant in death, sure that she has done enough to thwart the Dalek plans.

Countdown: TV show broadcast by the Games Station. This version gives contestants 30 seconds to disarm a bomb. The original version was the first ever show broadcast on Channel 4 in the UK.

Cronk Burger: Fast food of choice on Satellite Five (despite the reputation of the fourth great and bountiful human empire as the home of fine cuisine). The Cronk Burger can be eaten with cheese or with Pejatas, and costs 2 credits 20.

Crosbie: Unfortunate *Big Brother* contestant who is voted out shortly after the Doctor arrives.

Cyberman: The head of a Cyberman is seen in van Statten's alien museum. The Doctor greets the sight of his old enemy with some affection, commenting that it is 'the stuff of nightmares reduced to an exhibit'. Cybermen were, after the Daleks, the most enduring race of monsters from the classic years of *Doctor Who*. Originally humanoid, they replaced more and more of their body parts until they were more machine than human. The Cybermen are due to make their reappearance in the 2006 series of *Doctor Who.*

Daleks, The: The most famous of all *Doctor Who* monsters. Created as a result of genetic engineering on the planet of Skaro, Daleks are bred to be soldiers and have discarded every emotion except for hatred of all non-Daleks. The Doctor thought that they had been wiped out in the Time War, although at least two survived – one who fell to Earth and ended up in Henry van Statten's alien museum, and the Emperor Dalek who rebuilt a new Dalek army.

Davidge Pavel: Male programmer on the Games Station. He has secretly kept a log of all unauthorised signals coming from the station, which Jack uses to find the Dalek fleet. He dies during the final wave of the Dalek assault on the space station.

Davinadroid: Presenter of *Big Brother* on the Games Station. Voiced by real-life *Big Brother* presenter Davina McCall. Never actually seen on screen, although pictures of Davina are seen on the walls in the *Big Brother* house.

Delta Wave: A wave of Encasadine energy, which the Doctor plans to use to wipe out the Daleks. Jack says that it will barbeque the brain of anyone who stands in the way. Ultimately the Doctor can't bring himself to use it, because the cost of wiping out the Daleks would be to wipe out all of humanity as well.

De Maggio: A female guard in Henry van Statten's underground complex. She is ordered to get Rose and Adam safely away from the Dalek, and is killed when she decides to make a stand against it as it elevates up the stairs.

Diane Goddard: Assistant to Henry van Statten who is promoted early in 'Dalek' after her predecessor made the mistake of questioning his boss. Once the crisis of the Dalek escape is over, she stands up to van Statten and has his memory wiped, just as he had done to so many of his employees.

Doctor, The: The last Time Lord, a refugee from the last great Time War between the Daleks and the Time Lords. Known as 'the oncoming storm' in the legends on the Dalek homeworld. Our hero.

Editor, The: The highest ranking human employee of Satellite Five. He represents a consortium of banks with a financial stake in the plot to secretly enslave humanity.

Emperor Dalek: Somehow survived the Time War, and rebuilt the Daleks by stealing 'the prisoners, the refugees, the dispossessed' of humanity and growing new Daleks from the few suitable cells. Becomes convinced that it is a god, able to make new life. The Doctor says that it, and the other Daleks, have gone mad.

Face of Boe, The: The host of the party at the end of the world. Rumoured to have lived forever, and certainly possessed of extraordinary longevity far beyond the normal lifespan of its species. According to J.B. Dane (translated by Russell T. Davies in the BBC book *Doctor Who: Monsters and Villains*) if the Face dies 'then the sky will crack asunder. And it is said that he holds one, final secret; that he will speak this secret, with his final breath, to one person and one person alone. A homeless, wandering traveller . . .'

Female programmer: No name is given for this character. She dies attempting to fight off the Daleks in 'Parting of the Ways'. Previously she received short shrift from the Doctor when she tried to argue that exterminating thousands of humans was 'just doing our jobs'. Davidge Pavel is very fond of her.

Fitch: First contestant to be voted out on *The Weakest Link*. Rose votes for her.

Floor 500: The control level of Satellite Five (aka The Games Station). The walls are made of gold, apparently.

Fourth great and bountiful human empire: Supposedly the ruling power on Earth by the year 200,000. The Doctor says that they have spread out into the universe, mixed with other races and established themselves as the central point of their part of space. But the attentions of first the Jagrafess and then the Daleks throw the great and bountiful human empire off its correct path of development.

Gabriel Sneed: A Cardiff undertaker from the 1860s. His shop is located on the site of the rift between Earth and the dimension of the Gelth. He is killed by an animated corpse.

Gafabek: A foodstuff from the planet Lucifer, mentioned in a question in *The Weakest Link*. Rose thought it came from Mars.

Games Station, The: Home of such popular TV classics as *Big Brother*, *The Weakest Link* and, of course, *Bear With Me*.

Gelth: Gaseous creatures who lost their bodies due to the effects of the Time War. They use a space-time rift to attempt to occupy dead bodies and take over the world.

Georgian Road: Original location of Pete Tyler's death in 1987.

Graham Norton: Presenter of BBC TV's *Celebrity Dance Fever*. A mix-up in the feeds to BBC1 and BBC3 meant that noises from the *Celebrity Dance Fever* studio could be heard on three separate occasions in the first broadcast of 'Rose'. Graham Norton has since joked that he has updated his CV to include his appearance on *Doctor Who*.

Ground Force: TV show broadcast on the Games Station. Lynda describes it as being nasty – they turn you into compost. The original show featured gardener Alan Titchmarsh, along with co-hosts Charlie Dimmock and Tommy Walsh. There is no evidence of anyone being turned to compost, but Alan Titchmarsh did disappear from the show in 2002.

Gwyneth: A servant at Sneed's Funeral Parlour, she is also the key to the rift of the Gelth. She willingly agrees to make the bridge for them (believing them to be few, well-meaning and in danger), then willingly sacrifices herself in order to blow the Gelth up and thwart their plan.

Harriet Jones: MP for Flydale North who survives the destruction of Downing Street along with Rose and the Doctor, and who goes on to become Prime Minister, winning three general elections and becoming the 'architect of Britain's golden age' according to the Doctor. In the midst of the crisis, the Doctor tells her that she is 'very good at this'. It is Harriet who orders the Doctor to order the missile attack on 10 Downing Street.

Haverstock, Mr: The butcher who supplies Mr Lloyd with extra rations of meat in return for their homosexual liaisons. We never see Mr Haverstock onscreen.

Head Chip: Basic version of the Info-Spike. The basic head chip is fitted at the base of the skull and is practically invisible. It costs 100 credits and enables the user to interface with a simple computer.

Henry van Statten: Millionaire collector and entrepreneur living in the early twenty-first century. Van Statten collects alien artefacts, patenting the technology for profit, and suppressing advances that won't earn him money. He claims to own the Internet, and to be sitting on a cure for the common cold.

Hoob: A month in the pantraffic calendar. It comes before Pandol.

Hyper-Vodka: An alcoholic drink. Jack says he once ordered four of these for his breakfast when he was sentenced to death. He recalls waking up with both of his executioners, who have subsequently kept in touch.

Idris Hopper: Personal assistant to Margaret Blaine. Admits to the Doctor that Mrs Blaine is climbing out of the window.

Indra Ganesh: Aide to acting Prime Minister Joseph Green in 'Aliens of London'. When Rose, the Doctor and Harriet Jones discover his body, they are saddened to realise that nobody knows his name. It's Indra Ganesh. If only they had access to a copy of this book!

Info-Spike: Advanced form of head chip which enables journalists to process news stories on Satellite Five, effectively becoming computers themselves as they download and broadcast terabytes. Adam's cost him 10,000 credits, and it activates every time anyone clicks their fingers. He now avoids jazz clubs.

Isop Galaxy: A question in *The Weakest Link* asks who its oldest inhabitant is. Rose guesses (correctly) that it is the Face of Boe. The Isop Galaxy has previously been visited by the Doctor in the story 'The Web Planet' (1965).

Jabe: A tree from the Forest of Cheem. She recognises the Doctor as a Time Lord, and sacrifices her own life to help the Doctor save everyone else on Platform One.

Jack Harkness: A former fifty-first-century time agent turned intergalactic con-man who joins the crew of the TARDIS. Left the Time Agents once he realised that a two-year period of his memory was completely missing. Is the last to die as the Daleks storm the Bad Wolf Corporation space station in 'Parting of the Ways', but is brought back to life by Rose. The TARDIS leaves without him at the end of the episode. When the Doctor welcomes him into the TARDIS at the end of 'The Doctor Dances' Jack remarks, 'Bigger on the inside', to which the Doctor retorts, 'You'd better be.'

Jackie Collins: Author of the book *Lucky* (1985) and the answer to a question in *The Weakest Link*. Rodrick got it wrong, claiming the book was written by Jackie Stewart (a Formula 1 world champion from the 1970s).

Jackie Tyler: Rose's mum. Survives the Autons' killing spree in the shopping centre. Flirts with the Doctor when they first meet. Subsequently accuses him of putting her daughter at risk. Although she doesn't want Rose to travel with the Doctor, she borrows a breakdown truck to help Rose get back to him in 'Parting of the Ways'. Best understatement about the Doctor: 'He's good in a crisis, I'll give him that.' She does a lot more screaming than her daughter.

Jagrafess: The editor-in-chief of Satellite Five, who is enslaving humanity via manipulation of the media. The Editor says that his full name is 'the mighty Jagrafess of the Holy Hadrojassic Maxarodenfoe', or 'Max' for short.

Jamie: The original gas mask person. Jamie was killed in an air raid, and was repaired by the nanogenes, who lacked enough information to do more than a botched job. As a result all human life was threatened. Once everything has been put right, the Doctor tells him that he's going to love pop music.

John Smith: False identity assumed by the Doctor in 'The Empty Child'. This is the name that the Doctor most commonly uses when 'the Doctor' won't do. This alias first appeared in the Patrick Troughton adventure 'The Wheel In Space' (1968), and has recurred sporadically since then. Coincidentally, in the very first episode of 'An Unearthly Child' (1963), the (fictional) band that Susan is listening to on her radio is John Smith and The Coalmen.

Joseph Green/Slitheen: MP for Hartleydale, and chairman of the parliamentary commission for the monitoring of sugar standards in exported confectionery. He has been killed and replaced by one of the Slitheen, who becomes acting Prime Minister during the alien spaceship crisis. He publicly asks the United Nations to release Britain's missile codes so that he can defend the world against the aliens' 'massive weapons of destruction', which they can deploy in 45 seconds.

Ken Livingstone: Real life mayor of London, blamed by a passer by for the alien spaceship that brings London to a standstill in 'Aliens of London'.

Kyoto: City in Japan. The Doctor, Rose and Jack had some kind of adventure there in 1336. We don't know what they did, but we are told that they only just got away. It was after this that the Trans-Mat beam brought the TARDIS crew to the various gameshows on Bad Wolf TV.

Linda with an i: *Big Brother* contestant who was evicted for damaging a camera.

Lloyd, Mr: Owner of the house that Nancy raids in 'The Empty Child' and 'The Doctor Dances'. He is 'messing about' with Mr Haverstock the butcher and getting extra rations of meat as a result. Nancy uses this information to blackmail him in return for her freedom and some wire cutters.

Lunar Penal Colony: The Doctor, Jack and Lynda are told that they are to be taken – with no appeal – here after breaking out of the games on the Games Station. This is a reference to the Jon Pertwee adventure 'Frontier In Space' (1973), where the Doctor is sent to the Penal Colony.

Lynda Moss: (Lynda with a y – not to be confused with Linda with an i) Contestant on *Big Brother* who escapes with the Doctor when he breaks out of the studio. Subsequently dies during the defence of the Games Station against the Daleks. The Doctor describes her as 'sweet'.

Mal Loup: The American newsreader in 'Aliens of London' and 'World War Three'. Her name is an approximation of 'Bad Wolf'.

Margaret Blaine/Margaret Slitheen: The MI5 official whose identity is assumed by Blon Slitheen in 'Aliens of London' and 'World War Three'. She later crops up as mayor of Cardiff in 'Boom Town', having teleported herself away from the missile attack on 10 Downing Street. There she oversees the Blaidd Drwg project – a nuclear power station with design faults that will enable her to complete her plan of destroying the world for financial gain. A cold-blooded killer who claims to be a victim of her upbringing, and is given a second chance by the TARDIS. See also *Blon Fel Fotch Pasameer-Day Slitheen*.

Matt Baker: A real-life presenter of children's TV show *Blue Peter* who appeared in 'Aliens of London' demonstrating how to make a cake that looked like the crashed alien spaceship.

Mauve alert: Universally recognised signal for danger. See also *Red alert*.

Max: See *Jagrafess*.

Mickey Smith: Rose's boyfriend, referred to by the Doctor as 'Ricky' or 'Mickey the Idiot'. Mickey is eaten by a wheelie-bin, captured and replaced by an Auton. He survives this, and is rescued from the Nestene Consciousness. Subsequently, under instruction from the Doctor, he hacks in to both the UNIT and the Royal Navy websites and orders the missile attack that blows up 10 Downing Street. Later, he travels to Cardiff to meet up with Rose, the Doctor and Jack in 'Boom Town', and then helps Rose to rejoin the Doctor on the Games Station in 'Parting of the Ways'. Mickey is initially hostile to the Doctor, mistrusting the fact that the Doctor is alien, but they gradually develop some mutual respect.

Moonlight Serenade: The Glen Miller number which Jack plays while dancing with Rose on the bonnet of his spaceship. This tune previously featured in 'Revelation of the Daleks' (1985), played by Alexei Sayle's DJ.

Moxx of Balhoon: One of the guests at the party at the end of the world. He represents the firm of Jolko and Jolko Solicitors. The Moxx is blue skinned with pointy teeth, a large head, and has only four digits on each of his four limbs.

Mystery of Edwin Drood, The: The novel that Charles Dickens was writing when he died. In 'The Unquiet Dead', Dickens speculates that the Gelth could provide the ending that he has been looking for, and suggests renaming it *The Mystery of Edwin Drood and The Blue Elementals*.

Nancy: Young girl who finds food for the homeless children in Blitz-struck London. Finally revealed to be the mother (not, as she claimed, the sister) of Jamie, the dead child brought back to life by the nanogenes, an act of mercy which resulted in the strange space plague.

Nanogenes: Chula technology used by Captain Jack to heal Rose's hands after her escapade with the barrage balloon in 'The Empty Child'. More significantly, when they are released on earth they first encounter a dead boy, Jamie, wearing a gas mask. Their attempts to restore him to life are hampered by not knowing what he is meant to be like, and the result is a human/gas mask hybrid which threatens to remake all human life in its own image. When the nanogenes recognise the genetic similarities between the boy and his mother Nancy, they are able to undo their mistakes and, just for once, everybody lives – much to the Doctor's delight.

Nestene Consciousness: Alien life-form who comes to Earth because the high levels of toxins in the atmosphere make it a suitable planet for colonisation. Their own planet was destroyed by war – presumably the Time War referred to in later episodes. The Nestene Consciousness has the ability to control plastic, and appeared in two *Doctor Who* adventures in the Jon Pertwee era – 'Spearhead From Space' (1970) and 'Terror of the Autons' (1971).

Nul Points: The Doctor's assessment of the Daleks' attempt to exterminate him. The reference is to a score of zero in the *Eurovision Song Contest*.

Nurse: An employee of Satellite Five who persuades Adam to have the high-tech implant to enable his brain to interact with computers in 'The Long Game'.

Oncoming Storm, The: Legendary Dalek name for the Doctor.

Pakoo, Mr and Mrs: Guests on Platform One for the destruction of the Earth.

Pandol: A month in the pantraffic calendar. It comes after Hoob.

Pantraffic Calendar: The subject of a question on *The Weakest Link*.

Patrick Moore: Veteran presenter of BBC TV's *The Sky At Night* astronomy programme since 1957. When the Doctor asks Rose, 'Who's the biggest alien expert of them all?', Patrick Moore is her first guess.

Peace, Mrs: The dead woman possessed by a Gelth at the beginning of 'The Unquiet Dead'. She had a ticket to see Charles Dickens at the theatre, which is where the Doctor first encounters her.

Pete Tyler: Rose Tyler's Dad. He died on 7 November 1987. In 'Father's Day' Rose travels back in time and saves him from the car which was meant to end his life. As a result all human life is put at risk from Reapers who are attracted by the wound to time. He eventually realises what is happening and sacrifices his life so that everyone else can be saved.

Polar Ventura: Icelandic city which hosted *Murder Spree 20*. Rose thought it took place in Reykjavik. As if.

Price, Sergeant: Armed police officer on duty at 10 Downing Street during 'World War Three'. He is the one who gives the warning that there is an incoming missile attack.

Raxacoricofallapatorius: Home planet to the Slitheen family, a peaceful world which looks harshly on the criminal activities of the Slitheens, and has sentenced the entire family to a slow, painful death.

Reapers: Temporal creatures let loose on the Earth when Rose causes a wound in time by saving her father's life in 1987. The Doctor says that they are like a bacteria who have come to heal the wound by consuming everything inside it. He also says that if the Time Lords were still alive, they would have dealt with the Reapers. In the end they disappear once Pete Tyler allows himself to be run over by the car that was meant to kill him, putting time back on its correct path.

Red alert: Only the humans regard red as a signifier of danger. To all other species red has camp connotations, which the Doctor says gives rise to all sorts of misunderstandings.

Redpath, Mr: The first person to be killed by a Gelth-possessed body, in his case that of his grandmama, Mrs Peace.

Rick Astley: 80s pop singer whose record *Never Gonna Give You Up* is playing on Pete Tyler's car radio in 'Father's Day' before time distortions cause the set to retune anachronistically to The Streets.

Rodrick: Contestant on *The Weakest Link*. Votes tactically to keep Rose alive until the final, because he is confident that he can beat her. He does, and is still complaining about not receiving his prize money when the Daleks arrive. Refused to join Jack's force of volunteers to defend the Games Station from the Daleks.

Rose Tyler: A shop assistant from modern day London who stumbles upon the Autons, and becomes involved with the Doctor. In 'Parting of the Ways' she looks into the TARDIS' Time Vortex and becomes, for a time, a godlike being of immeasurable power. She can dance too.

Ruffalo: A plumber on board Platform One. She is the first victim of the Spiders as they seek to sabotage the party at the end of the world.

Sarah Clark: The bride at the wedding interrupted by Reapers in 'Father's Day'. She was marrying Stuart Hoskins.

Satellite Five: Home of *Bad Wolf TV*, the news broadcast service operated by the Jagrafess.

Sato, Doctor: The doctor who first examines the 'alien' in 'Aliens of London'. She does not realise that it is a genetically engineered pig, because the rewiring of the pig's brain is so far beyond the capabilities of any science known on Earth at that time.

Shadow Proclamation: The Doctor invokes convention 15 of the Shadow Proclamation when approaching the Nestene Consciousness to ask it to abandon the invasion of Earth.

Simmons: Employee of Henry van Statten's who tortured the Dalek. Once the Dalek uses Rose's DNA to regenerate, Simmons is the first to die, suckered to death.

Slipstream Compression Technology: Used by the Slitheen to impersonate humans.

Slitheen: Not a race of aliens, more a family business. The Slitheen are exiles from Raxacoricofallapatorius, and make their living by asset-stripping planets. The Doctor foils their plot to reduce the Earth to a nuclear wasteland and sell off the radioactive remains to the highest alien bidders. The Slitheen use slipstream compression technology to pose as humans (although only very big, fat ones). When so disguised they have a tendency to break wind uncontrollably.

Soft Cell: 1980s electro-duo consisting of singer Marc Almond and keyboardist Dave Ball. Their cover version of the Northern Soul classic *Tainted Love* is played at the party at the end of the world, and was the biggest selling UK single in 1981.

Sonic Screwdriver: The Doctor's all purpose home-made tool. It first appeared in the Patrick Troughton story 'Fury From The Deep' (1968), was lost by Peter Davison's Doctor in 'Visitation' (1982) and reappeared in *Doctor Who: The Movie* in 1996.

Sonny Hoskins: Father of the groom in 'Father's Day'. We first see him trying to persuade Stuart not to get married. When the Reapers appear outside the church, he makes a run for it and is quickly picked off. When Pete Tyler dies, Sonny reappears along with everyone else.

Spiders: Scuttling sabotage devices used by Cassandra in an attempt to destroy Platform One.

Spock: The alias Rose 'invents' for the Doctor when introducing him to Jack. When the Doctor had refused to do a scan for alien technology in 'The Empty Child', preferring to just ask people, Rose complained that he never 'gave some Spock'. The reference is to a character from the original series of *Star Trek*, *Doctor Who*'s main rival for the title of most popular long-running science fiction TV show. *Star Trek* was launched in 1966, some three years after the beginning of *Doctor Who*.

Stars in their Eyes: TV show broadcast by the Games Station. Lynda says that if you refuse to sing, you are blinded. The original version of the show was hosted first by Lesley Crowther, then Matthew Kelly and subsequently by Cat Deeley. Nobody was blinded, but several members of the audience may have wished they were deaf.

Stella Popbake: Fashion designer famous for hats and mentioned in a question in *The Weakest Link*.

Steward of Platform One, The: The person in charge of the smooth running of the party to watch the destruction of the Earth. Is killed when Spider sabotage lowers the sun filter in his office, leaving him unprotected against the intense heat of the expanding sun.

Streets, The: Musical alias of Mike Skinner. The Streets' 2002 single *Don't Mug Yourself* is heard playing on Pete Tyler's car radio once time becomes wounded as a result of Rose saving Pete's life.

Strood: Contestant on *Big Brother*. He complains when the Doctor arrives, arguing that adding somebody new after nine weeks isn't fair.

Stuart Hoskins: The groom at the wedding interrupted by Reapers in 'Fathers Day'. He was marrying Sarah Clark.

Suki: Real name Eva St. Julienne, a terrorist working undercover at Satellite Five in 'The Long Game'. Eva is a member of the Freedom 15, and the Editor says that she is 'a self-declared anarchist'. She is killed by the Jagrafess, and subsequently put to work on floor 500.

Suzie: Bridesmaid at Stuart and Sarah's wedding in 'Father's Day'.

Time War: The not so final confrontation between the Time Lords and the Daleks. The war had an effect on a number of races – destroying the Nestene Consciousness' protein planets and disembodying the Gelth for example – as well as wiping both the Daleks and the Time Lords from space and time – or so the Doctor thought. It is implied throughout the series that the Doctor was not only involved, but was the one whose actions led to the destruction of both Daleks and Time Lords. He tells the Nestene Consciousness that it wasn't his fault, and he is called a coward by the Daleks.

Trans-Mat: Device for transporting matter from one location to another. The device features in several *Doctor Who* adventures, from Patrick Troughton's 'The Seeds of Death' (1969) to Sylvester McCoy's 'Remembrance of the Daleks' (1988).

Tribophysical Waveform Extrapolator: A pan-dimensional surfboard, which Margaret Slitheen intended to use to escape from Earth when the Blaidd Drwg power station blew up.

Trine-e: Robotic co-host who attempts to give Jack a makeover, and gets more than she bargained for when he revealed his hidden (don't ask where from) compact laser gun. Voiced by, and modelled on presenter of *What Not To Wear* Trinny Woodhall.

UNIT: The United Nations Intelligence Taskforce. The Doctor describes them as 'good people' in 'Aliens of London'. When the Doctor was stranded on Earth in the Jon Pertwee era of the show, he was attached to UNIT as a special advisor. The last adventure where the Doctor joined forces with them was 'Battlefield' (1989).

University of Mars: Educational establishment in the year 200,000. Adam makes it up, claiming to be on a research project. It seems he chose well, as the nurse on floor 16 has no difficulty in believing that they could have made the mistake of sending a student with no head chip to Satellite Five. Or perhaps all universities are like that in AD 200,000.

University of Rago Rago Five Six Rago: Chosen scholars from class 55 are present on Platform One to witness the destruction of Earth.

Vomit-o-matic: Device installed in Adam's head as a special offer when he was fitted with an Info-Spike. Nanotermites are placed in the lining of the throat ready to freeze the waste if he is sick. It means that Adam now vomits ice cubes – watch your drink if you are ever at the same party as him.

Wipeout: TV show broadcast by the Games Station. The original was hosted first by Bob Monkhouse, and then taken on by Paul Daniels.

Zaphic: Drink sold by the fast food vendors on Satellite Five. Rose describes it as being like a slush puppy, but 'sort of beef' flavour.

Zu-zana: Robotic co-host who attempts to give Jack a makeover, and gets more than she bargained for when he revealed his hidden (don't ask where from) compact laser gun. Voiced by, and modelled on presenter of *What Not To Wear* Susannah Constantine.

Appendix 2:
Further Back in Time

The Doctor, wonderful chap, all of them
The Brigadier in 'The Five Doctors' (1983)

This appendix is primarily for the benefit of anyone who has discovered *Doctor Who* through the 2005 version and wants to explore the classic years of the show. There were 159 separate adventures broadcast from 1963 to 1989. Many of these, particularly from the Hartnell and Troughton eras, have fallen victim to the BBC's once haphazard approach to archiving material, and were lost or destroyed. All of the adventures that we recommend below are available on either video or DVD.

The list below does not represent a definitive list of 'best' *Doctor Who* stories. Rather this is a personal selection of recommended viewing – adventures that capture the qualities that made *Doctor Who* great, and which the authors of this book think are worth your time. We have also tried to get a reasonable spread of Doctors and companions, although inevitably there are some notable omissions.

Doctor Who fans rarely agree on the relative merits of different adventures, and we are no different. There were many good natured but strongly argued discussions that led to the compiling of this list, and some instances of unilateral vetoing of particular stories. This accounts for the relatively small section given over to Sylvester McCoy's years as the Doctor, and indeed the non-appearance of Paul McGann's only official trip in the TARDIS. These absences reflect in no way upon the quality of either actor, or their performances as the Doctor, but do illustrate what we see as a decline in the overall quality and consistency of the show as a whole. Having said that, there are many episodes in the McCoy era with excellent elements to them, and the one that we do recommend is a classic that stands shoulder to shoulder with the best of his predecessors.

So, if you want to explore the vast hinterland of *Doctor Who*, you could do a lot worse than to pick and choose from the following. They are listed in chronological order (of broadcast, rather than of time period visited). Enjoy.

William Hartnell (1963–66)

The Dalek Invasion of Earth (1964)
The second appearance of the Doctor's greatest foes, and the first instance of a companion (Susan in this case) leaving the TARDIS crew. This story was the basis for the second of the Peter Cushing *Doctor Who* films.

The Time Meddler (1965)
A good example of the old-style historical stories of the Hartnell era. Also the first big-name guest star (*Carry On* actor Peter Butterworth) and the first time that the Doctor encounters another of his own species (although the words 'Time Lord' were not to appear for another four years).

Patrick Troughton (1966–69)

Tomb of the Cybermen (1967)
The Doctor, Victoria and Jamie join an expedition which uncovers more than they bargained for. What could be lurking in the mysterious frozen tombs on the planet Telos? Hint, the adventure isn't called 'Tomb of the Accountants'. A welcome return for one of *Doctor Who*'s most enduring monster races.

The Mind Robber (1968)
A quirky delight, as the Doctor, Jamie and Zoe find themselves trapped in a world of make believe. Watch for the skilful last minute script doctoring to get around a tight recording schedule and a key member of the cast going down with chicken pox.

The War Games (1969)
A worthy final hoorah for Patrick Troughton. We finally discover that the Doctor is a Time Lord, and the excitement doesn't drop for all of the ten – count them – episodes. Jamie and Zoë and a host of future *EastEnders* actors (well, two at least) try to keep up.

Jon Pertwee (1970–74)

The Daemons (1971)
The Doctor and UNIT lock horns with two mighty foes: a demonic alien called Azal and the Pertwee era's recurring villain of choice, the Master. 'The Daemons' often features strongly in polls for the best ever *Doctor Who* adventure – who are we to argue?

Carnival of Monsters (1973)
Petty beaurocrats, ducking and diving entertainers, and aliens – including the Doctor and Jo – miniaturised and trapped in a machine. Look out for an appearance by actor Ian Marter, who would soon return to the show to play companion Harry.

Planet of the Daleks (1973)
Regarded by one of the authors of this book as the best Dalek adventure of them all. This has Pertwee's Doctor at his moralising best, and using the contents of his pockets to get out of a locked cell. All this and invisible aliens, the largest army of Daleks ever seen (until 'Parting of the Ways') and Jo falling in love.

The Time Warrior (1973–1974)
The first appearance of long time companion Sarah-Jane Smith, and also of highly popular monsters the Sontarans. The Doctor solves the mystery of disappearing scientists and runs amok in medieval England.

Tom Baker (1974–81)

The Ark In Space (1975)
The Doctor waxes lyrical about how great humans are, and tries to save us all from being turned into giant space insects. Sarah-Jane and Harry tag along for the ride, and bubble wrap has never looked so menacing.

Genesis of the Daleks (1975)
The Dalek origins story, mark II. Forget everything William Hartnell told you, and glory in the maniacal genetic jiggery-pokery of Davros. This, his first appearance, is highly effective, but his recurring presence in later adventures got a bit annoying.

The Talons of Weng Chiang (1977)

Baker is streets ahead of the police with this Sherlock Holmes inspired Victorian murder mystery. Dodgy special effects of giant rats, but a first class story featuring a criminal refugee from Earth's future, a Chinese magician and his evil pig-brained homunculus.

Horror of Fang Rock (1977)

The traditional 'base under seige' storyline handled expertly by *Who* veteran Terrance Dicks. An isolated lighthouse, an unnatural fog and the long-awaited appearance of the Rutans – mentioned for years as the other side in the war with the Sontarans.

Nightmare of Eden (1979)

A flawed gem. Despite the poor costume design of the Mandrels, Tryst's comic European accent and one moment of pantomime-like ham acting from Baker ('my arms, my legs, my everything!'), this still has much to commend it. Lalla Ward's version of Romana and K9 are the companions.

Peter Davison (1981–84)

Earthshock (1982)

Comedy legend Beryl Reid is cast superbly against type as a hard-bitten spaceship captain. Unfortunately for her, a Cyberman invasion force is lurking in her cargo hold. Good job that the Doctor, Nyssa, Tegan and Adric have come along for the ride too. Three excellent reasons for watching this – Cybermen back to their menacing best; an explanation of how the Dinosaurs died out; and the death of Adric, perennial contender for most unpopular companion ever.

Warriors of the Deep (1984)
The Doctor, Tegan and Turlough take on the combined might of the Silurians and the Sea Devils, two ancient and noble races last seen (separately) in the Pertwee era. Features Davison's classic 'There should have been another way' moment.

The Caves of Androzani (1984)
Shades of *Phantom of the Opera*, (but, happily, without Andrew Lloyd-Webber) and a genuinely sympathetic evil genius masterminding everything. Davison's final appearance shows his Doctor at his heroic best, giving his life to save companion Peri and running around in mines dodging androids. What more can you ask for?

Colin Baker (1984–86)

Vengeance on Varos (1985)
The Doctor transforms the economy of a struggling planet in the grip of an all-consuming media – twenty years before Russell T. Davies gave us the Bad Wolf Corporation.

Revelation of the Daleks (1985)
Littered with big-name guest stars, this is a creepy and enthralling adventure despite the fact that the Doctor is superfluous in plot terms. Eleanor Bron, William Gaunt, Alexei Sayle and that bloke from *Keeping Up Appearances* (Clive Swift) in a toupee. For once in the later years of *Doctor Who*, the barrage of special guests is not at the expense of a decent plot.

Sylvester McCoy (1987–89)

Remembrance of the Daleks (1988)
Set primarily in two of the locations of the very first *Doctor Who* episode, Foreman's junk yard and Cole Hill School. A fine example of the McCoy era's intent on recreating the Doctor's sense of mystery, and a well crafted Dalek tale that would grace any season of the show.

Bibliography

Books about *Doctor Who*

Mark Campbell, *Doctor Who* (Pocket Essentials, 2005).

Andrew Cartmel, *Script Doctor: The Inside Story of Doctor Who 1986–1989* (Reynolds and Hearn, 2005).

Paul Cornell, Martin Day & Keith Topping, *The Discontinuity Guide* (MonkeyBrain Books, 2004).

Peter Haining, *Doctor Who, A Celebration: Two Decades Through Time And Space* (Virgin, 1983).

J. Shaun Lyon, *Back to the Vortex: The Unofficial and Unauthorised Guide to Doctor Who 2005* (Telos Publishing, 2005) .

John Kenneth Muir, *A Critical History of Doctor Who on Television* (McFarland & Company, 1999).

Justin Richards, *Doctor Who: Monsters and Villains* (BBC Books, 2005).

Justin Richards, *Doctor Who: The Legend Continues* (BBC Books, 2005).

Useful Websites

The Official Doctor Who Website: www.bbc.co.uk/doctorwho

Outpost Gallifrey: www.gallifreyone.com

Doctor Who on Television: www.physics.mun.ca/~sps/tv.html#1doc

Relative Dimensions: www.relativedimensions.co.uk/

The TARDIS Index File: http://tardis.wikicities.com/wiki/
Main_Page

Timelash.Com: www.timelash.com/

The Doctor Who Appreciation Society: http://serendipity.
drwho.org

Damaris: www.damaris.org/doctorwho

Selective Bibliography

Julian Baggini, *Atheism: A Very Short Introduction* (Oxford
University Press, 2003).

Paul Copan, *True For You, But Not For Me* (Bethany House,
1998).

Michael J. Behe, William A. Dembski & Stephen C. Meyer,
Science And Evidence For Design In The Universe (Ignatius,
2000).

R. Douglas Geivett & Gary R. Habermas, *In Defence of Miracles*
(Apollos, 1997).

Guillermo Gonzalez & Jay W. Richards, *The Privileged Planet*
(Regnery, 2004).

C.S. Lewis, *The Abolition of Man* (Fount, 1999).

J.P. Moreland, *Scaling the Secular City* (Baker, 1987).

Victor Reppert, *C.S. Lewis's Dangerous Idea* (IVP, 2003).

Gregory Stock, *Redesigning Humans: Choosing our Children's
Genes* (Profile Books, 2002).

Lee Strobel, *The Case for Christ*, (Zondervan, 1998).

Anthony Thacker, *A Closer Look at Science Fiction* (Kingsway,
2001).

John Tulloch & Henry Jenkins, *Science Fiction Audiences:
Watching Doctor Who and Star Trek* (Routledge, 1995).

Michael J. Wilkins & J.P. Moreland, *Jesus Under Fire*
(Zondervan, 1996).

Peter S. Williams, *I Wish I Could Believe In Meaning: A Response
To Nihilism* (Damaris, 2004).

Index

About the Authors

Steve Couch
Steve's earliest *Doctor Who* memory is of Jon Pertwee in 'Planet of the Daleks', which he was delighted to rediscover during the research of this book. Steve is the Managing Editor of both Damaris Books and the website www.relessonsonline. com. He is also the co-author (with Nick Pollard) of *Get More Like Jesus While Watching TV* (Damaris, 2005) and the series editor of the *Thinking Fan's Guide* books. He is married to Ann and has a son Peter. Like the Doctor, if there's one thing Steve can do it's talk.

Tony Watkins
Tony's first *Doctor Who* memory was of Patrick Troughton being replaced by Jon Pertwee. Tony taught physics and mathematics for several years before joining the Universities and Colleges Christian Fellowship (UCCF) as a staff worker. He has been with Damaris from its inception, and is Managing Editor of the www.culturewatch.org website as well as the author of *Dark Matter: A Thinking Fan's Guide to Philip Pullman* (Damaris, 2004). Tony is married to Jane and has three boys, Charlie, Ollie and Pip. Like the Doctor, Tony came first in jiggery-pokery.

Peter S. Williams
Peter's earliest *Doctor Who* memory is the glitter-haired androids in 'Destiny of the Daleks' (1979), and he recalls playing as a child on the same Portsmouth beach that saw the first Sea Devil invasion. Peter is Managing Editor of *The Quest*, Damaris' online database of philosophical and spiritual

thinking. He is the author of a number of books including *I Wish I Could Believe In Meaning*: *A Response To Nihilism* (Damaris, 2004) and travels the country presenting sixth form conferences on ethical and philosophical subjects. Like the Doctor, Peter gives the impression of knowing what's going on.

DAMARIS
www.DamarisBooks.com

"Relating Christian faith and contemporary culture"

Join Damaris and receive

Discounts on other products from Damaris Books and Damaris Publishing.

Access to Web pages containing up-to-date information about popular culture.

To find out about *free membership* of Damaris go to www.damaris. org

DAMARIS
www.damaris.org

The Quest
(CD ROM)

Your journey into the heart of spirituality.

Take your own route, take your own time, seek your own answers to the big philosophical and religious questions with this self-updating oracle for your PC.

The Quest grows as you search, with free updates automatically downloaded from the web.

www.questforanswers.com

"Relating Christian faith and contemporary culture"

Matrix Revelations

A Thinking Fan's Guide to the Matrix Trilogy

Editor Steve Couch (and featuring contributions from all three authors of _Back in Time_)

The first in the _Thinking Fan's Guide_ series, providing in-depth analysis of the ideas behind the _Matrix_ films written for fans of the films by fans of the films.

What is _The Matrix_?

Groundbreaking, innovative and much imitated, the _Matrix_ trilogy represents the most talked about cinematic experience in recent years. Unrivalled in uniting serious philosophical thought with serious box office. _The Matrix_, _The Matrix Reloaded_ and _The Matrix Revolutions_ occupy a unique place in popular culture.

Matrix Revelations examines the _Matrix_ phenomenon, with in-depth analysis ranging from the science fiction and comic book influences to the philosophical and religious themes that underpin the films.

www.DamarisBooks.com

Dark Matter

A Thinking Fan's Guide to Philip Pullman

Tony Watkins

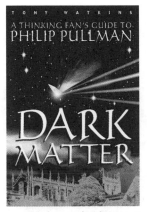

Another in the popular *Thinking Fan's Guide* series, exploring the major themes of Philip Pullman's *His Dark Materials* trilogy.

Philip Pullman's *His Dark Materials* trilogy is rightly acclaimed as a modern classic. Pullman creates alternative worlds that fascinate and delight, and has built up a loyal army of readers. He has been described as the 'most significant', but also the 'most dangerous' author in Britain. Who is Philip Pullman and why have his books provoked such a wide variety of strong opinions?

Tony Watkins explains what makes *His Dark Materials* such a magnificent work of fiction. He explores the influences that shaped Pullman's writing and the major themes of the trilogy including daemons, dust and Pullman's perspective on God.

www.DamarisBooks.com

I Wish I Could Believe in Meaning

Peter S. Williams

26.11.05

Wesley Owen
BOOKS MUSIC

£ 6.99

Peter S. Williams digs beneath our sceptical culture and invites us to take time out from the 'party' to seriously consider some of life's big questions – about truth, knowledge, goodness and beauty. He builds a convincing case for belief in meaning and purpose. In critiquing the arguments of zoologist Richard Dawkins he presents a serious challenge to naturalism. This book offers an alternative to atheism that addresses some of our deepest questions about life.

www.DamarisBooks.com